Black Women's Writing

Black Women's Writing

Quest for Identity in the Plays of Lorraine Hansberry and Ntozake Shange

Y.S. Sharadha

PRESTIG

Published by
Prestige Books
3/28, East Patel Nagar
New Delhi 110 008

ISBN: 81-7551-038-2

1998

Photo Typesetting by
Pivot Computers
Delhi 110 006
Ph. 2934490

Printed at
Chaman Offset Printers
New Delhi 110 002

Contents

For

My beloved parents

Srimati Y.S. Thulasi

Sri Y.S. Prathap Reddy

Preface

Lorraine Hansberry and Ntozake Shange, along with Alice Childress, are outstanding black women playwrights whose portraits of black life and culture are characterized by a vision distinctively feminine and different from that of many black male dramatists of the period. Childress, Hansberry, and Shange have shown the American Stage a multiplicity of images of female heroines and have not confined themselves to such limiting images of black women as immoral, promiscuous, wanton, frigid, overbearing, or pathetically helpless. They illuminate in general the condition of blacks in patriarchal America. The theatre which these dramatists have striven to create illustrates the existence of a black culture that continually invents itself outside the codes of the dominant society. The images of black culture and ethnic identity which Hansberry and Shange evoke in their plays acquire an added dimension on account of the black idiom which they employ in their plays. The focus is on a reassessment of black literature in an attempt to discover multiple black feminine styles.

One of the important features of African-American playwriting with special reference to Hansberry and Shange is that the problem of African roots engages the attention of these dramatists who portray in their plays a quest for identity. The drama of the discovery of African roots is enacted at the level of thematic unfolding and at the level of the dramatic design which includes miming, dancing, ritual, choreography, and other features derived from African ancestry and African world-view. The quest for identity leads these dramatists to evolve a theatre designed for the creation of a sense of the communal form and a theatre which is a monument built out of black awareness.

A study of the plays of Hansberry and Shange reveals how the black family is looked upon as dynamic cultural entity whose dialectical relations with other elements of the community and with the dominant society are the subject of dramatization. Hansberry's *A Raisin in the Sun* provides the most interesting prototype of the black family. She endows the Younger family with characteristics that challenge the existing stereotypes. Moreover, with her attempts to trace the past of women through tangles of heritage and personhood and with her memory anchored in the African soil, Hansberry offers a rediscovery and reinvention of African-American cultural heritage and identity.

Poet, playwright, and novelist, Ntozake Shange, a black feminist, emphasizes the importance of the choreopoem as a new genre in the American theatre and as a form rooted in an African tradition of movement, song, music, and emotional catharsis. As a black artist and a black feminist, Shange champions the woman of colour as she moves toward optimal self-consciousness, positive self-identity, and self-realization in an oppressive and blatantly sexist and ractist modern society. She expounds the metaphysical dilemma of being alive and being a woman and being coloured.

I have relied considerably upon the vast and fascinating body of writing on the African-American playwrights. My indebtedness to these sources is acknowledged in the book. Thanks to two study grants provided by the American Studies Research Centre, Hyderabad, I was able to consult important books and periodicals available at the Centre. I must, however, confess that even at the American Studies Research Centre some materials were hard to come by. The plays of Alice Childress, for example, were not all available except one or two which could be got at from collections of American plays. Hence the study could not make sufficient use of the Alice Childress material in spite of the fact that she formed with Lorraine Hansberry and Ntozake Shange a crucial link in the chain of African-American playwrights.

I express my grateful thanks to my research supervisor, Dr. C.R. Visweswara Rao, Professor of English, Sri Krishnadevaraya University, Anantapur, for his valuable suggestions and guidance. My sincere thanks are also due to Professor A. Ramakrishna Rao and all the other members of the staff of the Department of English for their encouragement and scholarly advice.

I have great pleasure in expressing my gratitude to my sisters, Y.S. Nirmala and Y.S. Bharathi, and my brother Y.S. Venkat Reddy, for their warm encouragement and loving kindness all through.

My thanks are also due to Sri Gangadhar, Library Assistant, S.K.University, and Sri Lokanna, Typist, for their help in the preparation of the thesis.

I shall fail in my duty if I do not express my appreciation and gratitude to Prestige Books for bringing out this book so elegantly and expeditiously.

Lorraine Hansberry and Ntozake Shange: Quest for African-American Identity

Black Americans today recognize more clearly than at any other time in their history that theatre as an institution can have a significant impact on the relentless struggle of a deprived racial minority for full equality. They recognize further that theatre promotes the need for spiritual wellbeing of a people divorced from their ancestral heritage through centuries of degrading slavery. This trend is clearly visible in the spectacular growth of Black theatres across the country. The term "black theatre" means theatrical production by blacks that serves as a tool for research into ethnic identity. It is also the most appropriate means for an analysis of the situation of blacks in North America for symbolic expression of the black world view and experience. As an ethnic theatre it is born out of historical conflict. At the heart of its beginnings is the quest for identity.

Genevieve Fabre contends in *Afro-American Poetry and Drama* that the 1950s saw the definite emergence of black playwrights. She points out that William Branch's *A Medal for Willie,* Alice Childress's *Trouble in Mind* (1955), Lorraine Hansberry's *A Raisin in the Sun* (1959), and Loften Mitchell's *A Land beyond the River* (1957) are among the best known plays by black playwrights of the 1950s.[1] In a majority of these plays protest is voiced, but violence as a solution is dismissed. The message in several of these plays, however, is that violence may soon become the only possible course of action. Mance Williams argues in *Black Theatre in the 1960s and 1970s* that "plays during the 1950s expressed a new form of protest, one that not only exhorted Black people to stand up for their rights but warned whites that Blacks would settle for nothing less than their full share of the American Dream."[2]

The 1960s saw a more radical militant theatre with Amiri Baraka at its head. Williams has observed: "whether playwrights of the 1960s fell into the category of realism or naturalism, Marxism or structuralism the prevailing mood of the period was that of revolt, outside and inside the theatre."[3] James Baldwin's *Blues for Mister Charlie* asserts that Blacks will remain victims as long as they depend on white liberals to free them from racial injustices. Like Baraka and Baldwin, Hansberry in *The Drinking Gourd* and Childress in *Wedding Band* express anger, disappointment, and a sense of helplessness. Though less overtly violent than Baraka's plays, the works of Childress and Hansberry are an outgrowth of the militant tradition. Their black characters are assertive, caustic, and unyielding to the demands of the whites. Other playwrights of the revolutionary theatre include Sonia Sanchez and Martie Charles whose plays advocate that blacks disassociate themselves from the decadant white society and its values.

A close examination of the plays of black women between the 1950s and 1980s reveals that though they treat many of the same themes as black male dramatists, their vision is different. Unlike their male counterparts, Childress, Hansberry and Shange have brought to the American stage a multiplicity of images of female heroines and have not confined themselves to such limiting images of black women as immoral, promiscuous, wanton, frigid, overbearing, or pathetically helpless. Peopling their plays with heroines who are challenging and innovative, Childress, Hansberry and Shange are important figures in the development of black playwriting and thus warrant serious critical study. A study of the symbols in selected plays by Childress, Hansberry and Shange reveals a shared vision: blacks must struggle together to secure political, social, and economic gains. What emerges as one examines the symbols in these plays is a conscious effort on the part of these dramatists to illuminate the condition of blacks in patriarchal America. In this "Theatre of Struggle" where battles are frequent, black resiliency and spirit of survival are heralded.

Two occurrences marked a revolution in black theatre in America and ushered in the Harlem Renaissance. First, in 1910, the National Association for the Advancement of Coloured People (NAACP) was formed. In that year the first issue of *Crisis* was published. Black artists could now publish their works, and even win literary contests. *Crisis* served as a laboratory for novice playwrights. Soon the NAACP's Drama Committee of Washington D.C. was established to encourage black playwrights to develop their craft.

The second occurrence that some critics say sparked the Harlem Renaissance was Ridgely Torrence's New York production in 1917 of *Three Plays for a Negro Theatre,* including *Granny Maumee, The Rider of Dreams,* and Simon the Cyrenian. This white playwright's interest in blacks as subject matter on the American stage opened the floodgates for black drama. The Negro became popular material for such writers as Eugene O'Neill, William Vaughn Moody, Marc Connelly and Paul Green. Responsible for the popularization of the primitivistic motif, these playwrights served as an impetus to African-American playwrights who began creating their own images of black men and women in an attempt to eradicate stereotypes of well-meaning white playwrights.[4] This emphasis on primitivism and exoticism resulted in the relegation of blacks to the musical rather than to the serious dramatic stage. Both black and white playwrights selected musicals as a medium. Between 1910 and 1940 over eight hundred musicals featuring blacks were produced.[5]

Before 1914, Blacks appeared in plays whose roles were enacted by the whites focussing on song, dance, and humour. In the black musicals or Coonshows, farcical caricatures of blacks were noticed. Between 1914 and 1930, the image of the new Negro emerged. This was the beginning of the cultural and intellectual awakening. Marcus Garvey, Bessie Smith and Langston Hughes were some of the pioneers of these new developments.

Early in American drama, white playwrights used misshapen Black images to help justify slavery. In the post-Civil War period, they used them to rationalize the nation's unfair treatment of blacks. Consequently, slaves were often portrayed as livings in an idyllic state. Free Blacks were seen as wretched in their freedom. The comic shenanigans of Black servants on stage indicated their happiness in the role of servitude. Blacks of both sexes were considered exotic primitives. Some white playwrights fashioned their own "truths" about Blacks. It was against such distortions as these that Black playwrights militated, out of necessity. Black humanity, for the most part, had to be proved to whites. But the "proving" has not been easy. Theatrical producers, who are usually white and male, are interested in scripts that promise commercial, if not critical, success. Plays about the Black experience articulated from a Black point of view that is alien to traditional, middle-class, and usually white theatre audiences were not welcomed. Black playwrights suffered from this neglect as well as from a lack of adequately equipped stages. Added to this, there was the paucity of talented directors, technicians, actors and actresses, and audiences. It has been mainly in community and university theatres catering to Black people, theatres reflecting a general consensus about the Black experience, that Black playwrights have been given a chance to grow.

While neither Black men nor Black women have had any real blow in the American theatre, Black women playwrights have had to contend with the additional onus of sexism. This was because playwriting has been regarded as a profession for men. With all the barriers of racism and sexism arrayed against them, some Black women writers have chosen drama as the form in which to express their creative talents. Before

1940, the suggested cut-off date of the Harlem Renaissance marked by the publication of Richard Wright's *Native Son*, there were a number of black women playwrights who felt compelled to speak their minds and express their hearts.6 Unlike many white women dramatists, however, "who wrote, like the (white) men with whom they competed, whose serviceable melodramas, farces, mysteries and (romantic) comedies . . . made up the season during the teens and expansive twenties," black women playwrights began writing serious drama, characterized most frequently by racial and social protest.[7]

During the years between 1916 and 1935, nine black women playwrights captured the lives of black people as no white or black male playwright could. Angelina Weld Grimke, Alice Dunbar Nelson, Georgia Douglas Johnson, May Miller, Mary Burrill, Myrtle Smith Livingston, Ruth Gaines-Shelton, Eulalie Spence and Marita Bonner were all original voices that were unwelcome in the commercial theatre of the period. These authors are crucial to any discussion of the development of black playwriting in America because they provide the feminine perspective and their voices give credence to the notion that there was a "New Negro" in America. The nine black women playwrights mentioned are indeed the heart of the Harlem Renaissance. They wrote mainly one-act plays about middle class and common folk, about passion and apathy, love and hate, life and death, hope and despair, self-effacement and race pride, oppression, and equality of the races and sexes.

With DuBois's *Rachel,* the theatre became a means of propaganda of racial awareness. After the second world war, Black theatre struggled to survive and black protest themes became rare. Lorraine Hansberry and Jean Genet revived black drama in the late 50s and early 60s projecting the blacks as real people with real concerns and problems. The focus is on the discovery of a black aesthetic. With Maulana Karenga setting the ground for cultural ideologies, a common black culture was sought after because without this, these ideologies would only be a set of reactions to whites and no more. Plays during the 1950s expressed a new form of protest, one that not only exhorted Black people to stand up for their rights but warned Whites that Blacks would settle for nothing less than their full share of the American Dream. Ironically, it seemed immaterial to angry Blacks—whether they were committed to non-violence or violence—that the American Dream was in a state of deterioration.

The efforts of the Black women forerunners helped to illuminate the way for later playwrights. The Civil Rights Movement of the 1950s and 1960s and the Black Consciousness Movement of the late 1960s and early 1970s sensitized some members of the white theatre audience to dramas by and about Blacks. There was an increase in Black theatre audiences who expected to see authentic dramas about Black life. The Black Theatre Movement of the 60s and the 70s was a Populist Movement under the influence of which, rather than Black Revolt, an evocation of black consciousness was sought to be projected. This is quite in contrast to the defeatist psychology which prevailed earlier and which was conditioned by the history of enforced servitude, discrimination, and racial denigration.

One of the first Black women playwrights to attract attention during this period was Alice Childress. Like her predecessors, Childress in her first published play, *Florence* (1950), used the one-act form.[8] In the waiting room of a rail-road station in the South her principal character, a Black woman of low economic circumstances, undergoes a change of mind through a chance encounter with a white woman. Instead of going to New York city to bring Florence, her fledgling actress daughter, home, the Black woman sends her travel money to the young woman so that she can remain in the city, continue to pursue her career, and perhaps succeed. In the play the newly 'liberated' white woman is having a chat with a black acquaintance, whose daughter is trying to break into show business in New York City:

> Mama: Could I ask you something?
> Mrs. Carter: Anything . . .
> Mama: Florence is proud . . . but she's having it hard . . . Could you help her out some, mam? knowing all the folks you do . . . may be . . .[9]

Ironically, Mrs. Carter offers to help by getting a friend who is a director to hire Florence as a domestic: "I'll just tell her . . . no heavy washing or ironing . . . just light cleaning and a little cooking . . . does she cook?"[10] By forcing the reader/audience to look at the injustice of black American life, Childress makes us aware of the many sides of racism and prejudice, and challenges blacks as well as whites to change it.

In *Trouble in Mind* (1955), a full-length work produced in an off-Broadway theatre, Childress again focuses on a strong Black woman, a veteran of show business named Wiletta Mayer.[11] Wiletta objects to the unrealistic role she has been assigned to play in "Chaos in Belleville," a melodrama with an antilynching theme articulated from a white point of view. She knows that taking such a stand will result in her termination from the production. But she loves the freedom of giving vent to her long-repressed feelings about prejudice in the American theatre.

Wine in the Wilderness,[12] which sprang from the Black revolutionary period of the 1960s, brings together inner city and middle-class Blacks who learn about their identities with the help of a ghetto heroine named Tomorrow Marie. She is a contrast to the middle-class types who equate Blackness with such superficial trappings as rhetoric, use of the Black idiom, and African objects d'art, but who, in reality, are empty and artificial. What really matters, they learn in the course of the play, is what is inside a person.

Other plays by Childress include *Mojo* (1971) and *String* (1971). In *Mojo,* a two-character play whose theme is Black love, a serious illness motivates a divorced woman to visit her former husband who is now involved with a white woman, and they rediscover each other.[13] In *String* (1971),[14] a short play based on Guy de Maupassant's story entitled "A Piece of String," an innocent man with odd habits is accused falsely of theft at a Black Neighbourhood Association picnic in New York City. Interspersing comedy and sadness, Childress treats the timeless subject of dignity. And in *Wedding Band* (1973),[15] a full-length play set in South Carolina in 1918, she focuses on romance between two quite ordinary people, who are, however, forbidden by law to love because one is white and the other Black.

Efforts to create a black theatre reached an important stage with the founding of the Federal Theatre Project (1935-39). Its first concern was to fight discrimination at all levels in the theatre and in the society at large. It protested against the persistent use of blackface, which excluded blacks from certain roles and left prominent actors unemployed. Basically the situation of the African-American theatre did not change much as a result of the FTP. After the demise of the Federal Theatre in Harlem, new community theatres arose that kept alive the dream of an authentic black theatre.

Undoubtedly the best known Black woman playwright is Lorraine Hansberry. Her play *A Raisin in the Sun* was staged on Broadway in 1959 and won critical acclaim and the New York Drama Critics' Circle Award as the best play of the 1958-59 theatre season.[16] With this production Hansberry became the first Black woman to have a play presented on Broadway. *A Raisin in the Sun* is perhaps the most famous play written by a Black American. Lena Younger, who has presided over her Chicago household since the death of her husband, hopes to bring to fruition her family's long-deferred dream of purchasing a home with light and space enough for everyone. Her husband's legacy—his insurance money—acts as a catalyst, projecting the family into a situation that not only causes dramatic conflicts but tests their character. The Younger Children—Walter Jr. and Beneatha—have dreams of their own. Walter, tired of chauffering and barely making both ends meet, wants to own his own liquor store, a dream that his mother cannot share partly because of her religious beliefs. Beneatha, a liberated woman interested in her African heritage, wants to be a doctor. Ruth, the daughter-in-law, a bit worn out on account of life's struggles, wishes to help her husband gain the "manhood" or self-respect he is seeking. She also acts as a peacemaker between the generations. Joseph Asagai, Beneatha's friend, dreams of a Black-ruled Africa. Hansberry in this play sets out to challenge existing stereotypes by retracing the important episodes in the history of this exemplary family. However, the situations in which the Youngers are placed and their behaviour show them to be exceptional and separate from the mass of family "types" in the ghetto. Instead of destroying the stereotype, the play only shows how the Youngers escape it.

Like those of many African-Americans, the Younger's forbears left for the North in search of employment and a life free from racism. As in *Our Lan'* by Theodore Ward, the family epic begins with dreams and hopes, despite inevitable setbacks. In the Chicago ghetto, the Youngers subsist in poverty. To make the relations between the characters more dramatic, Hansberry introduces a moment of crisis when each dreams of spending the dead father's insurance annuity in his or her own way. The different aspirations reveal diverging ethical choices and become sources of conflict.

No doubt, *Raisin* illustrates the social and racial relations in America which promises integration only in theory. On a more profound level, the Youngers' victory is due to the fact that they are different from others in the ghetto: they "deserve" to move into the white suburbs because they have adopted the values of the middle class that they hope to join. Hansberry's hope for integration for the Youngers' and for black theatre can pass as a concession to the tastes and ideology of Broadway audiences. The Younger family's aspirations—to get out of the ghetto at all costs, to satisfy basic needs and eventually "plant a garden"—characterize many ghetto families. But the Youngers' entry into an all-white neighbourhood does not portend a bright future. Pehaps it is on this point that the play is unsatisfactory in its depiction of integration as salvation. The test of blacks desiring to integrate into a white neighbourhood at the end of the fifties is depicted somewhat more realistically in *Take a Giant Step* by Louis Peterson. This play can serve as a follow-up to *Raisin* since it shows the life of a black family after the move. Yet neither Hansberry nor Peterson states openly that integration is often a trap for blacks.

The words from a speech made by Lorraine Hansberry to a Black Writers' Conference in New York City in 1959 provide an opportunity for us to rediscover the depth and breadth of Hansberry's social and political concerns. In her speech she says:

> I was born black and female. I was born in a depression after one world war, and came into my adolescence during another. While I was still in my teens the first atom bombs were dropped on human beings at Nagasaki and Hiroshima. And by the time I was twenty-three years old, my government and that of the Soviet Union had entered actively into the worst conflict of nerves in human history—the Cold War. . . . I have, like all of you, on a thousand occasions seen indescribable displays of man's very real inhumanity to man, and I have come to maturity, as we all must, knowing that greed and malice and indifference to human misery and bigotry and corruption, brutality, and perhaps above all else, ignorance—the prime ancient and persistent enemy of man—abound in this world.
>
> I say all of this to say that one cannot live with sighted eyes and feeling heart and not know and react to the miseries which afflict this world.[17]

What is most familiar in the above words is the sense of disbelief at what we, as humanity, will do to each other in the name of that same humanity.

Lorraine Hansberry was proud of being "young gifted and Black" at a time when Black women were stereotyped as merely long suffering matriarchs with sharp tongues. Her redefinition of black women as active and responsible participants in our political future was surprising in 1959 and remains so to some as we enter the 1990s. It is her pride and the scope of her vision that are the key to her uncommon consciousness. She saw that in order for a great work to be truly universal it had to be painfully specific. The truth of Black lives had to be explored, not recast into imitations of white life, before Black theatre would take its place in world drama.

A Raisin in the Sun opened up the questions of the validity of the middle-class aspirations, the right of women to control their own bodies and their intellectual independence, the inherent conservatism of the underclasses, the myth of the Black matriarchy, the connection between Africans and African-Americans some of which were issues not raised by Blacks in public. Because Hansberry has been regarded only within the light of Black—mostly male—dramatists, her larger context as a woman has been ignored. Discussion of *Raisin* is most often centred round Walter Lee and his frustrations or his conflict with his mother.

The character frequently overlooked is Beneatha, Walter Lee's sister, and the most autobiographical of Hansberry's characters. Early in the play Beneatha has this exchange with the African who is forcing her to marry him:

Beneatha:	You never understood that there is more than one kind of feeling which can exist between a man and a woman—or, at least, there should be.
Asagai:	(Shaking his head negatively but gently): No. Between a man and a woman there need be only one kind of feeling. I have that for you . . .
Beneatha:	I know—and by itself—it won't do. I can find that anywhere.
Asagai:	For a woman it should be enough.
Beneatha:	I know—because that's what it says in all the novels that men write. But it isn't.[18]

These words were not put in the mouth of Beneatha merely to show her as rebellious and troublesome. These are the political beliefs of Hansberry. In some unpublished notes she examines the idea that "feminine" traits such as love, compassion, and understanding are reserved for only woman's personality. Her understanding of the nature of relationship between women and men is further revealed when she says: "This is the supreme insult against men. It is only woman who truly possesses the most magnificent features of the human race—I a woman think not—and it is time men decided it is the great slander of the ages—to take our hands—truly as comrades."[19]

Blacks rejected the names given to them by White America. The term "nigger" became reminiscent of scorn and insult. The word 'Negro' lost the significance the Harlem Renaissance had given it. It came to symbolize a half-life accepted for too long. These were replaced by the word black. Family names, formerly given to slaves by their masters, were sometimes abandoned in favour of names of African origin freely chosen. It is interesting here to note that Genevieve Fabre traces the development of black playwriting itself to its earliest roots in Africa.[20] LeRoi Jones became Amiri Baraka, and Don L. Lee became Haki-Madhubuti. The idea of a black nation brought with it the possibility of a collective identity.

Five years after *A Raisin in the Sun*, Hansberry's *The Sign in Sidney Brustein's Window* (1964) appeared on Broadway.[21] In this work, Hansberry treats the private woes of Sidney, who is yet to find the right dream, and Iris, who is struggling to be liberated from the confining role that her husband has required her to play. The sign in Sidney's window indicates that he has been persuaded to campaign for a friend who is running as a reform candidate. A number of characters enter the home of Iris and Sidney. One of them, a Black man, eloquently articulates the pain of his race. At the end of the play, despite the dishonesty of the candidate he has supported and his gloom at the suicide of his sister-in-law, Sidney is moved to make something strong of this latest sorrow. Again, there is affirmation and hope. In *The Sign,* Hansberry has created a framework in which her characters could comment on the disorders and agitations of contemporary life. It is a drama of ideas rather than of action.

Among the unpublished plays of Hansberry is *Les Blancs,* whose final text was adopted by her literary executor and former husband, Robert Nemiroff, and produced on Broadway in 1970.[22] Set in a Mission compound—a hospital established in Africa by a European minister, seemingly suggested by Albert Schweitzer—and in the hut of a tribal elder, the play involves conflicting ideas during a period of change in Sub-Sahara Africa. The Blacks who once asked peacefully for freedom from the colonialists are now staging a revolution. The play focuses on three Black African brothers who espouse different attitudes to Africa.

In a sentimental unproduced fable, *What Use Are Flowers?* Hansberry depicts an old hermit who lived away from civilization for twenty years. The hermit finds some wild children who, before an unnamed holocaust, were brought to the edge of the forest by someone who wanted the human race to continue.[23] The hermit sets about the uneasy task of teaching these children the rudiments of civilization. Before he dies, one of them invents the wheel .

Of Hansberry's unproduced plays, the most interesting is *The Drinking Gourd* which was commissioned by the National Broadcasting Corporation.[24] While the work reveals the horrors and cruelties of slavery, it is in Hansberry's own words, "a serious treatment of family relationships by a slave owning family and their slaves."[25] With her attempts to discover the past of women through tangles of heritage and personhood and with her memory anchored in the African soil which evokes images of a distinctive character, Lorraine Hansberry offers a rediscovery and reinvention of African-American cultural heritage and identity.

For blacks in exile, Africa is a memory anchored in the collective consciousness more than in actual reality. Although this memory is transmitted from generation to generation, black Americans are under pressure to construct a cultural form made up of different behaviours and customs. Black culture in America is not African but African-American developed in response to the requirements of a new environment. The plays and theories of Paul Carter Harrison[26] participate in the debate on blackness and Africanness. For Harrison the theatre is an arena where the destiny of blacks can be staged. It is a privileged environment where art can save the ethos of a people and restore these peak points to African-American culture.

African distinctiveness appears most strongly in religious life and in music and dance. Harrison sees expressions of African experience in popular culture through song, sacred or profane, dance, and drum music symbolized by that eminently African instrument. These are the components of black sensibility and cultural heritage which the artist must know. The role of the theatre is to revalidate the spirituality of black America, to revive the collective race memory by retaining remembrance of slavery, and to reinstate an African vision of the world. Harrison refuses western theatre because it restricts free expression of black creativity. He rejects the theatre of the oppressed victims because its use of social realism shows only one side of human relations.

In order to develop the artistic and ideological basis for a new drama, black theatre establishes strong ties with African-American culture. Combining the three principles of drum, song and dance, the theatre associates textual with scenic writing and performs functions that were once held separate in the other arts. From the Harlem Renaissance to the sixties, theoreticians of black art have always placed culture at the heart of this debate. As an instrument for reflection and analysis, theatre is viewed as a continuous means to rediscover and reinvent the cultural heritage. African-American drama is often constructed round the double perspective of destroying the foreign code imposed by the dominant ideology and developing its own more relevant system.

The black renaissance of the sixties called for a theatre of "black experience" as well as one of struggle. The theatre was no longer dependent on white liberals or black militants. It was created from the most fundamental aspects of African-American life. Ron Milner's 1968 essay "Black Theatre—Go Home"[27] makes a plea for this. He calls upon his fellow playwrights to create a living art from materials and techniques within the community. The preference is for an art free from Western tradition and renewed by contact with black people. Ed Bullins in *Village Voice*[28] points out that the theatre is a monument built from black awareness and it is a sanctuary for the recreation of the black spirit.

Because the oral tradition has long remained a living practice in African-American culture, the dramatic artist has been tempted to emulate not only the art and techniques of the storyteller but also his prestigious social function—that of recording and reformulating experience, of shaping and transmitting values, opinions and attitudes, and of expressing a certain collective wisdom. Many folklore heroes—Slave John or the trickster fighting against hypocrisy and power, the bad man who fears neither God nor the Devil—serve as archetypes for theatre protagonists. They question the validity of stereotypes of blacks while demonstrating the oppressed people's refusal to become victims. Finally, the hero is often a teller who builds up his own character and transforms his companions into listeners. Thus at the core of its structure the theatre recreates a narrative situation.

Black music also contributes to the creative process. From early on the message, which even the revolutionary ideology of the sixties could not fail to hear, was that through music black people affirmed their ability to control chaos, confer meaning on absurdity and restore spirituality to the universe. Spirituality of soul, the governing principle of this music, is both a strategy and an aspect of character, a conscious and active step in bringing about change.

With the diversity of black women's lives now acknowledged in literature, African-American women writers search for new ways to express old and new situations and silences. Using blues and jazz, black urban speech, contemporary music, history, science fiction, dreams, magic and the mundane, these women speak out in their own characteristic way.

One of the forms frequently used in black literature is the blues. The blues has been the underlying ingredient of most popular music today. But its importance lies not only in sound, but also in its relationship to the history of a people. Amiri Baraka explains thus: "The term blues relates directly to the Negro, and his (her) personal involvement in America. Blues means a Negro experience, it is the one music the Negro made that could not be transferred into a more general significance than the one the Negro gave it initially."[29] Langston Hughes was the first poet to recognize its power, and in the late 1970s African-American women writers also pursued its literary possibilities. By using this form as a basis for written expression, these writers have merged the old with the new and captured the essence of black tradition and culture. By doing so, they honour not only the beauty and resilience of black life but also the women who are the substance of their songs.

The blues, black America's spirited and often ironical statement of hard times, hopes and triumph, was first performed—and frequently written—by black women in the 1920s. These blues singers gave the music worldwide recognition and their profession gave them freedom and independence from back-breaking field work or domestic servitude.

An interest in Black culture during the 1960s created a critical interest in the past and culture of black women. There was a stage when the writings of African-American women were simply invisible in the development of black literary history by males. Robert Bone's *The Negro Novel in America* betrays, according to Barbara Smith, "white racist pseudo-scholarship."[30] As a result, Black women critics have had to reconstruct the African-American literary tradition to include women writers and also eradicate stereotypes of black femininity and myths about black women's roles. The focus is on the cultural importance of black women writers and on a reassessment of black literature and literary history in an attempt to discover multiple black feminine styles.

As Toni Cade Bambara says, "in order to do justice to the survival techniques, psychic or economic, of black women in their community black writers have to adopt an interdisciplinary approach mixing accounts of songs, writings and oral history."[31] This is a pattern distinctly visible in the innovative theatrical style of Shange. Writers like Audre Lorde and Alice Walker have in the later day developed the themes of black feminist criticism and black writing. These writers see the study of black woman in literature as part of that larger study of expression in black behaviour. In the case of Shange what is particularly appealing is how language operates in her writing and how she re-works it to support a whole culture.

According to Mikhail Bakhtin's notion of dialogism and consciousness, each social group speaks in its own "social dialect" expressing shared values, perspectives, ideology and norms. These social dialects become the "languages" of heteroglossia. If language for Bakhtin is an expression of social identity, then subjectivity is constituted as a social entity through the role of the word as the medium of consciousness. Consciousness, then, like language, is shaped by the social environment. "Consciousness becomes consciousness only . . . in the process of social interaction."[32] Bakhtin further defines the relationship between consciousness and *inner speech*. He says that consciousness becomes a kind of inner speech reflecting "the outer world" in a process that links the psyche, language, and social interaction. If black women speak from a complex social, historical, and cultural positionality which constitutes black female subjectivity, they express a certain dialogics of discourse which provides an appropriate model for articulating a relation of mutuality and reciprocity. This is a pattern which we notice in the evocative theatre of Shange. The language of Shange develops its own linguistic signs of expression. In fact, it is through such language that the black man captures private yet communal cultural rituals. This language employed in a dramatic context lends a polyphonic density to the ideas and *images of poetry.*

Ntozake Shange first came into public prominence with the production of her choreopoem, *For Colored Girls Who Have Considered Suicide/ When the Rainbow is Enuf* (1976). A startlingly new dramatic approach to black life, this 'play' comprises seven female characters (ladies in brown, yellow, orange, red, purple, blue, and green). Through poetry, dance, and song, they tell of their trials and triumphs in a world bent on their eradication and silence:

> ever since I realised there was someone calt
> a colored girl and evil woman a bitch or a nag
> i been tryin not to be that & leave bitterness
> in somebody else's cup/ . . .
> So this is a requiem for myself/cuz
>   i have died in a
> real way / . . . cuz i don't know
> anymore/how to avoid my own face wet with my
> tears/cuz i had convinced myself colored girls
>   had no
> right to sorrow/ . . .
> i cdnt stand it
> i cdnt stand bein sorry and colored at
>   the same time
> its so redundant in the modern world.[33]

The play received favourable reviews as well as scathing ones. Many black men were outraged at their portrayal as non-caring, violent oppressors. Although the male characters receive little psychological probing, the words of the women characters have been received by a large section of the black female audience with resounding applause. Shange's choreopoem is a theatrical expression that is distinctly of African-American heritage, in its arousal of an emotional response in the audience. It further emerges from an African tradition of story-telling, rhythm, dance, and emotional catharsis. One of the important points to note about the theatrical art of Ntozake Shange is that her work demands that inner rhythms be physicalized.

One of the first black feminist plays to speak honestly about the terrible rupture in male/female relationships and the denial of black women's voice in American society, *For Colored Girls* is an expressive and highly creative work. Shange's honest appraisal of black life can be seen in all her works. She explains the need to touch the deeper, less expressed emotions that we all carry around—in deliberate defiance of western notions of decorum:

> Our society allows people to be absolutely neurotic and totally out of touch with their feelings and everyone else's feelings, and yet be very respectable. This, to me is travesty. So, I write, to get at the part of people's emotional lives that they don't have control over the part that can and will respond.[34]

Shange's ties with black culture are evident in the musical idiom and the content of her work. They are also expressed in the way she re-invents English spelling and punctuation and its placement on the page. She explains this to Claudia Tate:

> It bothers me . . . to look at poems where, all the first letters are capitalized. That's why I use the lowercase alphabet. Also, I like the idea that letters dance. . . . I need some visual stimulation, so that reading becomes not just a passive act and more than an intellectual activity, but demands rigorous participation. Basically, the spellings reflect language as I hear it. I write this way because I hear the words.

It is words wedded to music and dance that Shange employs in her experimental theatre works, *Spell # 7* (1979) and *Boogie Woogie Landscapes* (1979). The first involves nine characters who gather in a bar to discuss their lives. All are black actors and actresses who expose the restrictions and racism of America's theatres. One of the women sums up their situations:

> & atleast yr not playin a whore/if some other woman comes in here & tells me she's playin a whore/i think i might kill her.[36]

The instancy of the effects communicated by the theatre-pieces on the stage is such that what is reflected on the stage is the audiences' experiential identification with the emotional responses to actions. It is thus that Neal Lester describes the theatre-pieces of Ntozake Shange as "extended poetry moments."[37]

Boogie Woogie Landscapes is the more experimental of the two. Shange here mixes surrealism and expressionism in a portrait of "nightlife companions" who sing, dance and share emotional moments as black women in America. The play is basically concerned with women's rights. One character makes a powerful statement on its behalf:

> It really is not so good to be born a girl when we have to be infibulated, excised, clitorectomized & STILL be afraid to walk the streets or stay home at night . . . monsters and rapists. They are known all over the world & are proliferating at a rapid rate.[38]

She manipulates language to achieve raw emotion like passion, rage, anger, resentment, ecstasy, and pain. About this, she says: "I am committed to the idea that one of the few things human beings have to offer is the richness of unconscious emotional responses to being alive. . . . [Y]ou cannot exclude any human being from emotional participation."[39]

A Photograph: Lovers in Motion (1979) is the third of the trilogy. It comes closest to traditional theatrical form using five characters who intertwine with each other's lives. The story concerns a black male photographer. He is pursued by the other characters who want some kind of sexual and/or emotional commitment from him, as he tries to become a worthy artist representative of his black culture.

Through her explosive and evocative work, Shange has placed her finger on the pulse of black women's lives in contemporary urban society. She has described *From Okra to Greens/A Different Kinda Love Story: A Play With Music & Dance* (1985) as a "feminist poem in motion."[40] Set within the framework of a variant of the boy-meets-girl love story. In the play, Okra (the black female) gives Greens (the black male) a gift—her sociopolitical views on the black woman's existence within the local, national, and international arenas. In one sense, Greens represents Shange's ideal black male, though his coming to know about the complex realities of female existence is a gradual process. When the choreopoem opens, Greens comments on the painful "crookedness" of the black woman's existence. His sensitivity to women's realities is described here:

> folks wd just play
> wit her/get their kicks
> watchin the crooked lady
> do her thing/& her bones
> gotta crackin
>
> shatterin/mutilatin
> themselves til she
> waz looking so weird
> to herself she
> locked herself up in
> a closet.[41]

Once Greens and Okra become sexually and then romantically involved, he becomes the black male who works to understand the black women's particular oppression. With this understanding, they are able to work together as a black couple against the racist society that victimizes them both.

Shange's theatre pieces deal with complex notions of identity. They present a range of experiences of blacks in general and black females and black female artists in particular. Transferring her own private experiences and political voice into a dramatic form that reaches across to a public audience, Shange demands that "a poem should fill up with something| could make you swoon, stop in your tracks, change yr mind, or make it up/a poem should happen to you like cold water or a kiss."[42]

Shange has perhaps been most misunderstood in her portrayal of black men. An examination of Beau Willie, Sean David, and Greens offer evidence that Shange's treatment of black men is not unilaterally hostile and dependent upon negative stereotypes. As E. Ethelbert Miller declares, "Ntozake Shange is not a radical feminist singling out men as the primary problem in our society; instead she is a Black artist opening our eyes to the totality of . . . (black women's) dilemma."[43] While her choreopoems celebrate black female identity, Shange at no point encourages women to eschew all social or intimate contact with men as the solution to male exploitation. She works toward a level of communication in male-female relationships that is built upon mutual respect, trust, and individual self-worth.

As an African-American woman feminist, an artist, Shange has shown on the American stage that black females are worthy of heroic stature and literary exploration. Showing that black women possess vast creative potential in their dramatization of their self-worth and self-realization in a sexist, racist and capitalist society, Shange creates an effective poetic drama, the form of which has been examined from formalist, biographical, historical and feminist standpoint.

A systematic exploration of black culture has allowed the theatre to uncover the principles of an ethos and the foundations of a drama. In militant theatre, the investigation of certain alienating aspects of the culture led to rupture. In the theatre of experience, a search for ethnic continuity legitimizes the culture.

The common basis of myth provides that Eliot calls an art form to the modern. It is a mode of dislocating language into meaning. In the context of African-American writing with special reference to Lorraine Hansberry and Shange, Eliot's definition of the auditory imagination seems to have a significant application. In his *The Use of Poetry and Use of Criticism* Eliot defines auditory imagination thus: "(It) is the feeling for syllable and rhythm, penetrating far below the conscious level of thought and feeling, invigorating every word; sinking to the most primitive and forgotten" and further it fuses "the most ancient, and the most civilised mentality."[44] The fusion of the ancient, that is, the rootedness in a mythic archetype and the modern is what gives the drama of Hansberry and Shange their special appeal.

Belonging as they do to the black theatre movement of the sixties and the seventies, Alice Childress, Lorraine Hansberry, and Ntozake Shange, concentrate on an evocation of black consciousness and heritage. The theatre for them seems to offer a revalidation of the spirituality of black America. The evocative use they make of music, song, and dance fuses the textual, the scenic and the archaeological. In their rediscovery and dramatization of African-American cultural heritage and identity, Hansberry and Shange could, in a sense, be described as literary anthropologists. Feminist criticism challenges the fundamental theoretical assumptions of literary history and criticism by demanding a radical rethinking and revisioning of the conceptual grounds of literary study that have been based almost entirely on male literary experiences. While white male-dominated writing is scripto-centric, black women writers define an alternative reality rooted in self, folk-tradition, and female bonding. Some of the implications of this revisioning have already been realised in African-American literature, as we can notice in the analysis of the works of Lorraine Hansberry and Ntozake Shange.

African-American theatre has reached a cross-roads in its evolution, and a double hypothesis can be presented about its future. First, this future is in the hands of a system of cultural production that has eliminated some former prejudices. Animated by liberal pluralism, the future is paving the way for different ethnic theatres. Secondly, the future of the black theatre is also in the hands of the black community as a whole, and not just the artists. The theatre is not only the creation of authors, actors and producers. It brings together the thinking and feelings of the community. If theatre is "an empty space to be filled," then this arena can become the place of lively dialogue only when all the elements that compose the theatre act are present. A truly ethnic theatre cannot survive without the concern and attention of its audience. Moreover, black theatre will survive only if a dialogue with the group is maintained and if the forms that support that dialogue are constantly renewed.

NOTES

Genevieve Fabre, *Afro-American Poetry and Drama 1760-1975* (Detroit,

Mich: Book Tower, 1979) 251-63.
2. Mance Williams, *Black Theatre in the 1960s and 1970s* (Westport, Conn.: Greenwood Press, 1985) 112.
3. Mance Williams, 113.
4. Sterling Brown, *Negro Poetry and Drama* (Washington DC: The Associates in Negro Folk Education, 1937) 115.
5. Alvin Goldfarb and Edwin Wilson, *Living Theatre: An Introduction to Theatre History* (New York: McGraw Hill, 1983) 433.
6. Arthur P. Davis and Michael W. Peplow, ed., *The New Negro Renaissance* (New York: Holt, Rinehart and Winston, 1975) xxi.
7. Helen Rich Chinoy and Linda Walsh Jenkins, *Women in American Theatre* (New York: Crown, 1981) 130.
8. Alice Childress, *"Florence," A One Act Drama, Masses and Mainstream,* 3 (October 1950) 34.
9. Ibid., 35.
10. Ibid., 38.
11. Lindsay Peterson, ed., *Black Theatre: A 20th Century Collection of the Work of Its Best Playwrights* (New York: Dodd, Mead, 1971) 135-74.
12. Alice Childress, *Wine in the Wilderness* (New York: Dramatists Play Service, 1969).
13. Alice Childress, *Mojo* and *String* (New York: Dramatists Play Service, 1971) 3-22.
14. Ibid., 25-50.
15. Alice Childress, *Wedding Band* (New York: Samuel French, 1973).
16. Lorraine Hansberry, *A Raisin in the Sun* and *The Sign in Sidney Brustein's Window* (New York: New American Library, 1966) 186-318.
17. From a speech delivered at a Black Writers' Conference in 1959. Qtd. *To be Young, Gifted and Black*, adapted by Robert Nemiroff (New York: New American Library, 1969) 41.
18. Lorraine Hansberry, *A Raisin in the Sun* (New York: New American Library of World Literature, 1959) 11-12.
19. Lorraine Hansberry's unpublished untitled notes, New York City, Nov. 16, 1955. Qtd. Margaret Wilkerson, "Lorraine Hansberry: The Complete Feminist," *Freedomways*, Vol. 19 (Number 4, 1979) 244.
20. Genevieve Fabre, *Drumbeats, Masks and Metaphor: Contemporary Afro-American Theatre* (Boston, Mass.: Harvard University Press, 1983) 4.
21. Lorraine Hansberry, *A Raisin in the Sun* and *The Sign in Sidney Brustein's Window*, 186-318.
22. Lorraine Hansberry, *Les Blancs: The Collected Last Plays of Lorraine Hansberry,* ed. Robert Nemiroff (New York: Vintage Books, 1973) 47-186.
23. *Ibid.,* 323-70.
24. *Ibid.,* 187-313.
25. *Ibid.,* 193.
26. Paul Carter Harrison. *The Drama of Nommo* (New York: Grove Press,

1972) 24.

27. Ron Milner, "Black Theatre—Go Home," *Negro Digest*, April 1968, rpt. Gayle, *Black Aesthetic*, 291.
28. Ed Bullins, "Manifesto," *Village Voice*, Nov. 1973, 60.
29. LeRoi Jones (Amiri Baraka), *About Blues, Blues People* (New York: William Morrow, 1963) 94.
30. Barbara Smith, *Towards a Black Feminist Criticism* (New York: Out and Out Books, 1977) 4.
31. Toni Cade Bambara, 'Commitment: Toni Cade Bambara Speaks,' *Sturdy Black Bridges: Visions of Black Women in Literature*, ed. R.P. Bell *et al* (New York: Anchor Press, 1979) 235.
32. Mikhail Bakhtin, "Discourse in the Novel," rpt. Michael Holquist, ed., *The Dialogic Imagination: Four Essays* by M.M. Bakhtin (Austin: University of Texas Press, 1981) 292.
    V.N. Volosinov (Mikhail Bakhtin), *Marxism and the Philosophy of Language* (New York: Seminar Press, 1973) 11, 29. This concept of the "subjective psyche" constituted primarily as a "social entity" distinguishes the Bakhtinian notion of self from the Freudian notion of identity.
33. Ntozake Shange, *For Colored Girls Who Have Considered Suicide/When the Rainbow is Enuf* (New York: Macmillan Bantam Books, 1980) 44-46.
34. Ntozake Shange, Interview with Claudia Tate, *Black Women Writers at Work* (New York: Continuum, 1983) 156.
35. Claudia Tate, *Black Women Writers at Work*, 163.
36. Ntozake Shange, "Spell # 7" in *Three Pieces* (New York: St. Martin's Press, 1981) 23.
37. Neal A. Lester, *Ntozake Shange: A Critical Study of the Plays* (New York and London: Garland, 1995) 6.
38. Ntozake Shange, "Boogie-Woogie Landscapes" in *Three Pieces,* 135.
39. Claudia Tate, *Black Women Writers at Work*, 151.
40. Ntozake Shange, *Southern Register*, 5 (Spring/Summer 1985).
41. Ntozake Shange, *From Okra to Greens/ A Different Kinda Love Story: A Play/with Music & Dance* (New York: Samuel French, 1985) 8-9.
42. "Ntozake Shange Interviews Herself," MS. (December 1977) 72.
43. E. Ethelbert Miller, "For ZAKI—who Dances the Bomba," *New Directions* (April 1980) 30.
44. T.S. Eliot, *The Use of Poetry and Use of Criticism* (London: Faber and Faber, 1933) 118-19.

A Raisin in the Sun: Quest for African Identity and Universality

Lorraine Hansberry revolutionized black theatre in America in 1959 when her play *A Raisin in the Sun* became the first play on Broadway by an African American woman. This trail-blazing play won for Hansberry the coveted New York Drama Critics Circle Award making her the fifth woman, the youngest playwright, and the first woman in America to be so honoured.[1] It is a play about what kind of conviction and commitment it takes to bring hope out of hopelessness, courage out of fear, and idealism out of fatalism. The play deals with a black family—the Youngers—and their ordeal of trying to move out of a segregated Chicago borough.

Commenting on the twenty-fifth anniversary production, the *New York Times* drama critic, Frank Rich, hailed *A Raisin in the Sun* as the play that "changed American theatre for ever" by forcing "both blacks and whites to re-examine the deferred dreams of black America."[2] He further said that the play portrayed all Hansberry's concerns about a black family "with a greater realism and complexity than had ever been previously seen on an American stage."[3]

A Raisin in the Sun celebrates both black culture and black resistance to white oppression through many generations. Hansberry says, "The thing I tried to show was the many gradations even in one Negro family the clash of the old and new but most of all the unbelievable courage of the Negro people."[4] The three generations of the Younger family depicted in the play differ in dreams, speech patterns and religious, musical and stylistic preferences within the African-American and African traditions, thus displaying the richness and diversity of black culture. Yet they are unified in their heroic defiance of white hostility and threats. The issue is not integration. The test that the Youngers face relates to their willingness to take potentially fatal risks to get out of an intolerable situation and to force change upon an oppressive system.

The dreams that Big Walter's family have about the insurance money's uses represent a cross-section of Black America's dreams that have been systematically suppressed by white racism. Walter Lee wants to enter business by becoming a partner in a liquor store. Beneatha attempts to develop her intellect and be of service to humanity by practising medicine. Ruth likes Travis to grow up in a decent home in a decent neighbourhood. Lena desires to save her family from the dissolution threatened by the internalized social and economic pressures embittering them all. Just as Shakespeare expanded the boundaries of the revenge tragedy of Thomas Kyd to include pressing political issues of his day as well as the most significant universal concerns, Hansberry stretched the domestic drama to include three hundred years of historical dreams and struggles as well as universal hopes and frustrations. The family in the play is the most extended one possible. All the generations of blacks brought to the United States are represented in the play in microcosm and through them finally all of humanity.

In the plays of Alice Childress, Lorraine Hansberry, and Ntozake Shange three images which appear most frequently are "the black male in search of his manhood," "the black male as a walking wounded," and "the evolving black woman." The black male in search of his manhood is shown either as a creature who is in the process of becoming a mature human being or one who is too incapacitated to search for manhood. Though he may reject his ethnicity during the search, he reaches maturity when he realizes that his manhood does not hinge upon his acceptance by anyone but himself.

In Alice Childress' *Mojo: A Black Love Story,* Teddy represents those black males who refuse to let poverty and bad luck keep them from growing into fine black men who accept responsibility for their families. The dual protagonists Lena Younger and Walter Lee in *A Raisin in the Sun* and the conflict centred on their differing ways of looking at the world are what give the play dramatic tension as well as intellectual and emotional appeal. In addition, this duality provides a structure that points to the tragedy of Walter's reach for the American Dream.

In the play there is a conflict involving the carfare Walter who needs to get to work as well as numerous other conflicts before and during the breakfast. Walter's comic, poetic, male-chauvinist lament, "Man say to his woman: I got me a dream. His woman say: Eat your eggs"[5] is one of the most memorable speeches in modern drama. Hansberry's accomplishment in the play thus reflects and matches her high intentions and gives it the same visionary force as Miller's *Death of a Salesman.*

Ironically, the positive qualities of character which should lend dignity to Walter's character such as his iron will, his high expectations of himself, and his determination to succeed, are those which reduce him to the role of a villain when he is compared to his mother. However, no real enmity exists between Walter and his mother. Though opposites in their ways of looking at the world and in their responses to it, they are united by love for each other and for their family. Both seek to improve the conditions affecting their lives.

Lena Younger's thinking is restricted by time. Her thinking is that of a Black woman born near the turn of the century in a racist American society. She does not understand the modern ways and thinking of her children. "Something has changed," she tells Walter:

> You something new, boy. In my time we was worried about not being lynched and getting to the North if we could and how to stay alive and still have a pinch of dignity too. . . . Now here come you and Beneatha—talking 'bout things we ain't never even thought about hardly, me and your daddy. You ain't satisfied or proud of nothing we done. I mean that you had a home; that we kept you out of trouble till you was grown; that you don't have to ride to work on the back of nobody's streetcar—You my children—but how different we done become. (62)

This statement makes clear that racial conditioning has had as profound an impact on her life as that of gender.

Mama's reflections on yesteryears provide the audience with insight into her tenacity. She had clung for nearly forty years to her dream of extricating her family from the ghetto. Mama's sense of family is expressed in her remarks to Walter, her son, and Beneatha, her daughter, about ingratitude and irreverence respectively. When Beneatha becomes iconoclastic, Mama reminds her that she and Big Walter brought her up in the church and that she had better remember the values and morals they tried to teach her. Mama is spiritually rooted in African-American culture and traditions.

Mama also teaches Beneatha a lesson when the young girl says that her brother is not a man but a toothless rat. She chastises Beneatha for thinking that she is better than Walter Lee. When Beneatha tells her mother that there is nothing left to love in Walter Lee, Mama instructs her that there is always something left to love. She teaches Beneatha that the time to love someone is not when that person has done good and made things easy for everybody, but "It's when he's at his lowest and can't believe in hisself 'cause the world done whipped him so." (136) In a very poignant moment, Mama cautions her naive daughter that when she starts measuring somebody, she should measure that person right by taking into consideration what hills and valleys that poor soul has traversed before getting to rock the bottom.

The fact that Mama carries her withering plant with her to the new house suggests that the weariness of living in America is not over but will be transferred to a new location. In spite of the uncertainty of their future, the blacks steadfastly celebrate the mending of a family that had literally been torn apart. Hansberry's aim is to capture the fervour of her characters' lives and demonstrate that they can survive whole in spite of all the responsibilities heaped upon the black woman's back. In the theatre, Hansberry could mirror not only the quagmires but the fullness of these women's lives. Wilkerson says of Hansberry, "The Theatre was a working laboratory for this brilliant woman whose sighted eyes and feeling heart caused her to reach out to a world at once cruel and beautiful."[6]

Lena's experience with discrimination as a young woman in the South affected her thinking. While they did not destroy her self-esteem, they did colour her outlook on life, narrowing her perspective and restricting her beliefs about what a Black person could reasonably expect to achieve in American society. The only way a Black person could escape discrimination in the South of that time was to move to the North. She is still a fighter, and proves it by buying the house to bring about the change she now feels is needed for her family's welfare. She says, "When the world gets ugly enough a woman will do anything for her family." (62) Her belief in this change, which is her version of the American Dream, sets her at odds with her son, Walter.

In short, Lena Younger's is not the true American Dream, but a version of it reserved for Black Americans and other poor people. But her dream is unacceptable to Walter who will have nothing less than the complete American Dream, since her version of it only amounts to surviving, not living in the fullest sense. Unlike his mother, Walter has managed to escape almost completely the crippling inferiority that destroys many Blacks, particularly men. What is most American about Walter and his thinking is his acceptance of American values, rather than stereotypes, myths, and untruths about Blacks, that enables him to dream and act in a typically American way.

Another source of Walter's strength is the fact that he is male. Lena Younger's world view and range of possibilities are restricted by her femaleness whereas Walter's are enlarged and enhanced by his maleness. A further source of strength lies in his belief in himself and in his ability to do what other successful Americans have done. He sincerely believes that he is cut out for better things. Near the end of Act II, scene 1, he describes himself as "a giant—surrounded by ants! Ants who can't even understand what it is the giant is talking about." (76) This strong faith in himself is the basis of his typically American self-reliance and rugged individualism.

Ironically, the influence of his own Black family and the values they believed in and lived by prepared Walter to accept mainstream American values and to strive to reach his goal. He was also influenced by outside forces existing in the society at large. These delicately balanced value systems provide the basis for the biculturality which characterizes the Afro-American. At the same time, this fact of biculturality underscores the two levels of universality inherent in the Black American experience. The dreams, hopes, and fears of the Younger family are universal reflections of those shared by people of all races all over the world. These are universally American aspirations.

Walter's image of his father matches the old stereotype of the hard working, long-suffering Black male who literally worked himself to death. Lena says:

> I seen . . . him . . . night after night come in . . . and look at that rug . . . and then look at me . . . the red showing in his eyes . . . the veins moving in his head . . . I seen him grow thin and old before he was forty . . . working and working and working like somebody's old horse . . . killing himself . . . (117)

There is no way Walter could forget this image, and the cheque becomes the symbolic representation of the senseless waste of his father's life. Other tangible signs of it are the cramped, roach-infested apartment, the shabby furniture, and the worn out rug on the floor. No matter how much he may have loved his father, it would be unthinkable to want to replicate his father's life. For this reason, the young white men of his age personify for him the true American Dream, a dream he knows he is worthy of:

> Mama—sometimes when I'm downtown and I pass them cool, quietlooking restaurants where them white boys are sitting back and talking 'bout things . . . sitting there turning deals worth millions of dollars . . . sometimes I see guys don't look much older than me. (61)

The stimulation that he gets downtown from seeing the young white men is quite different from that which he gets from the Black musicians at a Southside Chicago bar called the Green Hat:

> You know what I like about the Green Hat? . . . I like this little cat they got there who blows a sax. . . . He blows. He talks to me. . . . And there's this older guy who plays the piano . . . and they got a sound. . . . They got the best little combo in the world in the Green

> Hat. . . . You can just sit there and drink and listen to them three men play and you realize that don't nothing matter worth a damn, but just being there. (93)

The former source of stimulation invites action, while the latter induces inactivity. The actions of the young white men stimulate him to hope, dream, think, even scheme. Black music, on the other hand, becomes for him a kind of drug or narcotic that lulls him into a state of listlessness which allows him to escape depression.

Walter's personal stake in his dream is to be balanced by the primary purpose for which he seeks it—a radical change in his family's living conditions. This change is much wider in scope than Lena's planned move from their apartment and improved standard of living, a substantial move up the socio-economic ladder, the complete abandonment of poverty, and the chance to live the kind of life most Americans dream of living. The selflessness and nobility of this dream give Walter's character its dignity and spiritual dimension.

In making his decision to move into white neighbourhood, Walter acknowledges his links not only with his family but also with his race through the past, present, and future generations. He is moved not by a yearning to live near whites but by a refusal to let whites spit on his family's faces and also by a desire to obtain material basis for a good life for them in spite of whites. The plot reveals both the diversity of the family members seen as representatives of the African-American community as well as their unity and bravery in standing up to the insults, threats and near-certain violence.

Childress, Hansberry and Shange view black women from a special angle. One image which dominates their plays is "the evolving black woman," a phrase which embodies the multiplicity of emotions of ordinary black women for whom the act of living is itself heroism. Self-respecting, self-sufficient, and assertive, these women force others around them to recognize their adulthood. Beneatha Younger in the play typifies the evolving black woman. Though the daughter of one-time sharecroppers, Beneatha aspires to become a physician. In several speeches, she implies that becoming a doctor is far more important to her than finding a husband. She is professionally oriented and places no emphasis on entrapping a "bread winner." She is a young intelligent black woman who is aware of her capabilities and refuses to let anyone, including both her suitors, George Murchison and Joseph Asagai, minimize her potential.

Both George Murchison and Joseph Asagai, like Walter, are male chauvinists. They display traditional attitudes towards women, though in varying degrees. The middle-class American black, George Murchison, regards Beneatha's desire to be a doctor as laughable. When she tries to talk to him seriously, he advises her: "to cut it out, see—The moody stuff, I mean. I don't like it. You're a nice-looking girl . . . all over. That's all you need, honey, forget the atmosphere. Guys aren't going to go for the atmosphere—they're going to go for what they see. Be Glad for that." (88) Not surprisingly, Beneatha dismisses him as a fool.

Her other suitor, the African student Joseph Asagai, cannot be so easily dismissed since he is somewhat complex and highly appealing. His mixture of idealism and sophistication, his seeming role as spokesman for many of Hansberry's political and philosophical views, and his willingness to die either to free his country from colonialism or simply to aid its progress lend him the aura of a romantic hero. He is capable of such insensitive comments as "Between a man and woman there need be only one kind of feeling" and "For a woman it should be enough." (49) In spite of all his revolutionary attitudes, Asagai is, in this one area, a traditional—and fallible male. Unlike George Murchison, however, he is willing to listen to Beneatha and take her career goals seriously. He enables their relationship to grow thus and leaves open the possibility that he may eventually free himself of his remaining chauvinism.

Like Beneatha Younger, Florence in Alice Childress' *Florence*[7] is classified as an evolving woman. Florence is a positive image of black womanhood. She refuses to use racism as an excuse for not trying to improve her lifestyle. She represents those black women who refuse to despair in the sight of seemingly insurmountable obstacles. Instead of applying for public assistance, she sets out to become self-sufficient in a profession that she considers dignified. It is her determination to succeed which makes her a character to be admired.

The evolving black women in Childress' *Wine in the Wilderness*[8] and Ntozake Shange's *For Colored Girls Who Have Considered Suicide/When the Rainbow is Enuf*[9] are preoccupied with themselves because they have been disappointed by the men who came into their lives. These are women who have had their share of "deferred dreams." They are no longer willing to play the role of "Woman-behind-her-man" before men who appreciate neither their submissiveness nor their docility. These women rebel and claim that no man is ever going to oppress them again. They are not women who feel that all men are insensitive beasts. Instead, they are women who have become independent because of their fear of being abused physically or emotionally in subsequent relationships.

In spite of the special problems she has faced as a woman and other differences stemming from her education and idealism, Beneatha is essentially very similar to Walter. This similarity is accentuated in the stage directions which introduce her: she is "as slim and intense as her brother." (17) It is further emphasized by the way he shares her fantasy about being African. Moreover, she and her brother are both driven by egotism to get as much of the insurance money as possible for their personal goals. There is a similarity in their response to the loss of the money. Like Walter, she rises out of her despair to make an active commitment to the white-surrounded house, thereby gaining a corresponding sense of solidarity with her family.

All these resemblances suggest that men and women differ far less than traditional views would have us believe. Many of the "differences" are artificially induced by their cultures. Beneatha and Walter rightly come to see that their real opponents are not each other but the entire system of privilege and exclusion based on many false distinctions.

Hansberry's dual aim of demonstrating that the African heritage of black Americans is a glorious one and "that the ultimate destiny and aspirations of the African people and twenty million Negroes are inextricably and magnificently bound up together forever" is fulfilled in a variety of ways in *A Raisin in the Sun.*[10] Hansberry indicates the linkage in the stage directions by saying that Lena's "bearing is perhaps most like the noble bearing of the women of the Hereros of Southwest Africa." (22) Beneatha's willingness at the end of the play to entertain Asagai's proposal that she live with him in Africa suggests a symbolic as well as personal link between the blacks of America and those of Africa. In addition, Beneatha's intense reaction against anything smacking of whitewashed American culture, prompted in part by Asagai's "teasing" remark that her straightened hair reflects the "assimilation" of American blacks, (48) leads her to change to an Afro-hairstyle. She wears the African dress that Asagai has given her, plays African music on the record player, and attempts an African dance. By this Hansberry introduces her audiences to the beauty of all these vital aspects of African tradition.

Walter's drunken decision to join his sister in fantasizing about being African provides a comic interlude that has serious overtones, especially in regard to his relation to Africa. His first words upon taking on the role of the African are significantly, "YEAH . . . AND EHIOPIA STRETCH FORTH HER HANDS AGAIN!" (68) In his imagination Walter becomes one of those "fighters with spears" and starts "actively spearing enemies all over the room." (69) Moreover, he confirms his support for anti-colonialist struggle, like the one with which Asagai is involved in Nigeria, by saying, "Me and Jomo. . . . That's my man, Kenyatta." (69) This is a pointed allusion to Kenyatta's imprisonment by the Kenyan colonial government for agitating for independence. The poetic language Walter uses in his imaginary speech differs widely from his everyday speech. It is the kind he would have used as a leader in Africa. Its eloquence highlights the evocative language of the oral traditions of the Africans.

In *A Raisin in the Sun* Hansberry demonstrates a craft which is superior to mere skill in plot construction. With her awareness of the differing speech patterns of characters, which provide the specifics of their background through the language they use, Hansberry affirms the fact that the use of "black English" or "black English vernacular" is a legitimate part of the evocation of .African-American culture. Her lively delineation of widely contrasting speech patterns such as those of Mrs. Johnson, Lena, Beneatha, Lindner and Asagai show the immense range within even a single language in pan-African culture. It is significant that the most important speech defying the white attempt to keep blacks in their place is delivered by Walter. His announcement to Lindner that he and his family have decided to occupy their house is made in "black" English: "We don't want to make no trouble for nobody or fight no causes, but we will try, to be good neighbours. That's all we got to say." (138) In this context, Walter is saying that he refuses to be bought off. He is firm in his conviction that how he would act in future would depend on how the whites act. Walter's defiance expressed in "black" English indicates how Hansberry would defend the African-American idiom and the right to use the speech that most precisely expresses the emotions and experience of a people. In her essay, "The Negro Writer and His Roots: Toward a New Romanticism," Hansberry writes:

> The speech of our people has been the victim of hostile ears and commentary. That there are tones and moods of language that the African tongue prefers, escapes attention, when that attention would demand admiration of beauty and color rather than mere amusement or derision. The educated are expected to apologize for slurrings that haunt our speech; the mark of ascendency is the absence of recognizable Negro idiom or inflection. It is an attitude that suggests that we should most admire the peacock when he has lost his colors. Perhaps someday they will know it is not mere notes of music which command us—"When Malindy sings."[11]

It must however be borne in mind that Hansberry did not attempt to recreate the African-American idiom with the precision of a linguist. Like Mark Twain in *Huckleberry Finn*, she uses a modified form of speech that gives a realistic touch to her dialogue insofar as the nuances of vocabulary and patterns of speech reveal heritage and character traits. In fact, what Hansberry projects through the diversity of her black character's speech patterns and the uniformity of those of the white characters is the richness and complexity of African-American culture. In her attentiveness to the specifics of the culturally shaped speech, Hansberry depicts not only the breadth of African-American culture but also emphasizes that its language, society and art are not monolithic entities. This is exemplified by Lena, Murchison, Beneatha and others who in their speech patterns reveal their education and social levels, interests, and awareness of oppression.

Hansberry's interest thus is more comprehensive than an interest in the use of language for the creation of a realistic surface. By juxtaposing Beneatha's desire to return to the African tradition with the involvement of her mother and sister-in-law in African-American culture, she has not only delineated the diversity of black culture, but also expressed a viewpoint similar to that of Jordon who asserted that we must recognize "the need to abhor and defy definitions of Black heritage and Black experience that suggest that we are anything less complicated, less unpredictable, than the whole world."[12]

The arrival of George Murchison for his date with Beneatha and his distaste for what he regards as her reversion to the primitive afford Hansberry another chance to comment on African culture. George's speech derogating Beneatha's views on African heritage actually provides much positive information about Africa that Hansberry wishes to place before audiences: "In one second we will hear all about the great Ashanti empires; the great Sanghay civilizations; and the great sculpture of Benin and then some poetry in the Bantu and the whole monologue will end with the word *heritage*!" (72) He is opposed to a woman's "thinking." Black heritage to him "is nothing but a bunch of raggedy-assed spirituals and some grass huts." (72)

Asagai, a young Nigerian activist studying in America, is the catalyst for Beneatha's growing awareness of the need to fight for black people's rights and women's rights. Asagai teases Beneatha about multilating her hair by trying to straighten the beautiful curls made by Mother Africa. He brings her traditional African attire. But he suggests to Beneatha that she must not focus on the trivial blackness as expressed through garments but must work toward making blacks free to choose their destiny. He teaches her about striving for her own identity and independence as a woman and as a black. Accepting the call, Beneatha grows into a low level activist, one of the few black females to be designated as such in the literature of the period by black women dramatists.

Asagai, with his Western education and his strong and loving sense of the traditions of his people, is clearly the kind of African leader Hansberry depicts. He intends to bring many changes to his village and seeks to eliminate "illiteracy and disease and ignorance." But he feels that the ultimate judges of his actions must be his "black countrymen" and that if he does something profoundly detrimental to their way of life they would be justified in slitting his then useless throat. (124-25)

Hansberry uses Asagai as a symbol of black struggle and freedom. Asagai views himself as a liberator, a militant. He is consumed with thoughts of independence, as Beneatha notes. "All your talk and dreams about Africa and Independence. Independence and then what? What about all the crooks and petty thieves and just plain idiots who will come into power to steal and plunder the same as before—only now they will be black and do it in the name of the new Independence." (124)

Asagai insists that he plans to return to his country where he will lead a revolution against an oppressive white government. This brilliant young embodiment of the Black Power Movement in America and Africa poignantly reveals that he will go home to teach and work while activists plan and organize the revolution. He argues that there must be a revolution to rid his country of illiteracy, disease, and ignorance, which by the way are the same ailments that plague blacks and poor people in America. It is in this fusion of suffering of the blacks in both America and Africa that Hansberry shapes Asagai as the symbol of humanity's interconnectedness.

For Hansberry, the key to liberation for blacks in America and around the world is political power which could be attained through solidarity. Hansberry uses Africa in the play as a symbol of black struggle and freedom. Asagai, an African revolutionary, models for Beneatha the attitudes and commitment needed in order that blacks might secure full citizenship in America and the world. Asagai tells Beneatha that he would like to take her back to their ancestral home, Nigeria. He tells her that once they are home they would pretend that there were never three hundred years of separation. Hansberry makes it clear that African Americans and their counterparts in other parts of the world are a family who must unite in order to reconstruct a world that looks upon poeple of colour with hostile eyes.

The play's only white character is portrayed with humour and deliberately ironic juxtaposition. Hansberry makes Lindner's presentation of his mission dramatically ironic because everything seen of the Younger family defeats the "rational" core of Lindner's argument. His central point is that people are happier when they live in a community in which the residents share a "common background." From his viewpoint, "Negroes" and whites obviously do not have that common background. Hansberry has Lindner describe his community as a striking parallel to what the audience knows of the behaviour and desires of the Youngers: "They're not rich and fancy people; just hard working, honest people who don't really have much but those little homes and a dream of the kind of community they want to raise their children in." (103) Lindner's conniving dishonesty provokes disgust at his behaviour and applause for Walter's unhesistant refusal.

The character most neglected by the critics as also by the other characters in the play is Ruth. Her life is the most traditional, circumscribed and empty. It is a life of sacrifice and being sacrificed. She performs work that she hates for a woman whom she despises. She then comes home to a husband who neither berates her for not supporting him enough nor ignores her, and to a son who gives her affection but only limited respect. When she encourages Lena to use the insurance money to make a trip to Europe leaving the family behind and seeking fun for once in her life, she reveals her own longing for such a release. Ruth's outlet is vicarious pleasure in Beneatha's ability to break through many of the barriers that box Ruth in. That is why she is so willing to make financial sacrifices to help her sister-in-law. Like the other members of the Younger family, she is not prepared to die without fighting back, at least until the system has choked the breath out of her. The house represents her one chance at salvation. She clings to it fiercely, even when the others are ready to relinquish it. It represents her last hope to regain the attention between her and Walter, worn down as they are by the pressures of their lives.

A Raisin in the Sun is first and foremost a celebration of black life with all its diversity and creativity in speech, music, and other cultural forms and of black strength through generations of survival and struggle. Like Alex Haley's *Roots* published seventeen years later, the play depicts black values being passed on from generation to generation, with each generation adding its own contribution but retaining the wisdom and the will-to-freedom of its predecessors.

The Washington Post critic David Richards has argued that to view the play "memory in terms of evolving race relations or the class struggle, as some are wont to do, is to acknowledge only part of its greatness" and that "what makes 'Raisin' universal is Hansberry's fierce moral sense."[13] His argument has considerable validity. On the anti-integrationist side, Harold Cruse deplores *Raisin* as "the artistic, aesthetic and class-inspired culmination of the efforts of the Harlem left-wing literary and cultural in-group to achieve integration of the Negro in the arts." In other words, it is a "most cleverly written piece of glorified soap opera," a "second-rate" play about working class Blacks who "mouth middle class ideology."[14] This is a narrow view which denies the play its evocative power and its universality. The play contains generally acknowledged universal themes such as marital and generational discord, conformity versus respect for diversity, the struggle for women's rights, idealism versus cynicism, the dangers of misdirected ambition, and religious versus atheistic humanism. At the same time, these themes are linked inextricably to black experience and black perspective. Hansberry does not treat racial content and universality as though they are mutually exclusive. Instead, she implies that the underlying assumption that only the lives of whites have universal significance is another of the many racial misconceptions based on the inability of a large number of whites to view blacks directly. The point is that the specifics of the lives of blacks, carefully observed, are no less universal than the specifics of the lives of whites.

NOTES

1. Elizabeth Brown-Guillory, "Contemporary Black Women Playwrights: A View from the Other Half," *Helicon Nine: The Journal of Women's Arts and Letters,* Nos. 14 & 15, 1986, 121.
2. Frank Rich, "Theatre: 'Raisin in the Sun,' Anniversary in Chicago," *New York Times*, October 5, 1983: C 24.
3. *Loc. cit.*
4. Sylvia Danneth, *20th Century: Profiles of Negro Womanhood*. Vol. 2 (Yonkers, N.Y.: Educational Heritage, 1966) 262.
5. Lorraine Hansberry, *A Raisin in the Sun* (New York: Random House, 1959) 15.
6. Margaret B. Wilkerson, "The Sighted Eyes and Feeling Heart of Lorraine Hansberry," *Black American Literature Forum*, Vol. 17 (Spring 1982) 13.
7. In *Masses and Mainstream*, 3 (October 1950) 34-37.
8. In Hatch and Shine, *Black Theatre USA: Forty-five Plays by Black Americans, 1847-1974* (New York, 1975) 738-55.
9. (New York: Bantam Books, 1977) 3-64.
10. Lorraine Hansberry, "The Negro Writer and His Roots: Toward a New Romanticism," *Black Scholar*, 12.2 (1981) 2-12.
11. *Ibid.*, 7-8.
12. June Jordon, *Civil Wars* (Boston: Beacon Press, 1981) 85.
13. David Richards, "Shining 'Raisin in the Sun': At the Eisenhower, a Powerful Production of a Great American Play," *Washington Post*, November 17, 1986: D1, D8.
14. Harold Cruse, *The Crisis of the Negro Intellectual* (New York: Apollo, 1968) 278.

The Sign in Sidney Brustein's Window: A Play about Commitment

Lorraine Hansberry dedicates her second play *The Sign in Sidney Brustein's Window* to the committed everywhere. In doing so, she expresses her conception of the purpose of art. From the play it is evident that commitment does not mean for her what it meant for Brecht or even Rice and Odets. It does not also mean strong alignment with sectional interests which undermines the drama of LeRoi Jones. The commitment of which Hansberry speaks is to hope rather than despair and to human potential rather than human failure. Her enemy is thus neither the rich industrialist nor the racial bigot but rather the indifferent and the self-deceived.

The Sign in Sidney Brustein's Window is a more mature play than *A Raisin in the Sun.* The play offers a statement of artistic responsibilities as also of social inadequacies. The obligation to limit one's scope to the immediate but parochial injustices of racial intolerance has for long sapped the creative energy of the Negro writer. Having paid her debt to this tradition with *A Raisin in the Sun,* Hansberry achieves a significant break-through with *The Sign in Sidney Brustein's Window* which is clearly in the mainstream of contemporary drama. The Negro is no longer seen as the victim of a savage social situation. He becomes an endemic part of a society desperately searching for a valid response to the human condition.

The play is remarkable for not engaging in any direct fashion with the question of race and "difference," when such questions were uppermost in the minds of blacks.[1] The play does have one black character, Alton Scales. But his presence seems only to foreground the absence, as it were, of blackness as a motif. The play's unusualness is partly due to the dominance of white characters like Sidney Brustein, Sidney's wife, Iris, Iris's sisters, Mavis and Gloria, the playwright, David Ragin, and the politician, Wally. In addition, the chief character, Sidney is a jew. Hansberry's sympathetic treatment of a jew, the traditional enemy of the Black, is again a radical departure for a Black playwright. The play implicitly questions the methods of LeRoi Jones and Ed Bullins whose forceful and aggressive negation of White America is partly answered. In this play Hansberry is caught between her concept of drama as a means of a social statement and drama as an examination of character.

Sidney is a "big fat character" and he "monumentally" commands the play so that "we rise or fall" with him. John Braine affirms that "the play becomes Sidney Brustein's personal Odyssey of discovery, confrontation with others in the process of which he discovers himself."[2] As Braine's remark about Sidney's "personal Odyssey" implies, Sidney grows both in self-awareness and moral stature during the course of the play. However, what he learns and the decision he makes on the basis of this knowledge is the primary ethical content of the play.

Sidney is also the cultural centre of the play. Many cultures collide in Greenwich village. The people who enter Sidney's apartment represent an astonishingly wide variety of ethnic backgrounds. Sidney himself is jewish. His wife Iris is "the only Greco-Gaelic-Indian hillbilly in captivity."[3] His friends and aquaintances include Alton Scales (described by one character as a "cream-colored" black), Wally O'Hara (an Irish American "reform" politician who needs to be reformed), and Sal Peretti (an Italian-American juvenile junkie who worked for Sidney as a janitor and who died of an overdose of American oppression). The range of social backgrounds is similarly striking: Iris's sister, Mavis, is "The Mother Middle-class itself." (63) Her other sister Gloria is a call girl. Sidney's brother Manny is a successful businessman. Brustein's upstairs neighbour is a struggling, sponging, homosexual bohemian playwright, David Ragin, and their friend Max, "by all odds an original," (33) is an abstract but rather primitive painter who is not quite sure whether he prefers food or sex.

The range of the characters' cultural attitudes varies as widely as that of their backgrounds. Max insists on art for art's sake whereas Alton, an ex-communist who retains his belief in the ideals of Marxism, insists on art exclusively as an instrument of class struggle. Mavis believes that there is too much pain in real life and wants art to offer a peaceful escape while David strives for an art that presents only the agonizing part of life. Iris, although vocally "tolerant" of everybody, offers all sexual deviants, outcasts, radicals and weirdoes (in reality a single category for her) little compassion and even less understanding.

Sidney is the chief connection among all these cultural interests. One fundamental reason for Sidney's ability to perform this linking role is suggested by Ellen Schiff: "In making Brustein the axis of her play Hansberry draws on the historical experience of the jew. Her protagonist personifies an alien factor that has earned a degree of acceptance in society. Having accomplished that, he tends to regard race, creed and previous conditions of servitude largely as bothersome cliches and to devote himself to other pressing concerns."[4] Schiff also argues that Sidney is "one of the most successful characterizations of the jew on the post-1945 stage." And further, "a notably sensitive concept of the Jewish experience as archetypal furnishes the subtext of Hansberry's play."[5]

In effect this is an accurate picture of Sidney Brustein, as indeed it is of Arthur Miller's Quentin. For Sidney, in clutching naively at what he imagines to be innocence, becomes insensitive, blind alike to the crumbling of his marriage and the despair of his sister-in-law. His relationship with his wife, Iris, is strained because he refuses to recognise the reality of the world. But rather he chooses to remould it, and her, to suit his own personal vision. On the one hand he tends to lapse into a romantic dream of man as innocent and free spirit removed from the conventional corruption of the city. In this mood he takes *Huck Finn* as an archetype of noble dissociation and sees Iris as a mountain nymph. On the other hand he throws himself with naive faith into political activism. There is a bitter desperation in Iris's demand to know which role she should play—Margaret Mead or Barbara Allen—for her life is lived as a counterpart to her husband's. His sudden and impractical enthusiasms throw an increasing strain on their relationship. The crisis between Sidney and his wife is ultimately a crisis of Sidney's liberalism. For Iris rebels against the sterility of a life which gravitates around idealistic dreams a life of philosophical speculation and meaningless activity entirely lacking in a sense of commitment.

At the beginning of the play Sidney, who has just admitted to the failure of one of his impractical schemes, is prevailed upon to use a newspaper which he has bought to support a reform candidate in a local election. He accepts the campaign as a further diversion and the sign which he puts in his window (a sign pledging support for the reform candidate) is less evidence of his faith in the possibility of change than evidence of a self-justifying sense of the righteousness of protest. The Sign which hangs in Sidney Brustein's window is not an ironical comment on the impossibility of achieving anything in what Iris sees as this "dirty world."

> There are things talked about . . . laughed about while you stand there framed by that sign . . . that make me wonder how I ever thought you knew anything about this world at all. . . . *This* world, Sidney! It's so dirty. (116)

The Sign represents the public face of a man whose vision of the world is radically simplified. Until he is brought to the point of confrontation, he fails to understand what Hansberry conceives as the nature of commitment. The sign becomes, as Iris puts it to Sidney, "It's like spit in your face" (117)—a significant phrase carrying overtones of Miller's *All My Sons*. Sidney tells Mavis, his sister-in-law, that changing one politician for another "is to participate in some expression of the people about the way things are." (60) The act of protest is sufficient and when his candidate is elected he is genuinely amazed. For, as Hansberry suggests, Sidney's liberalism is the exercise of conscience without attendant responsibility. Indeed, he remains unaware, until informed by his wife, that he has secured the election of a candidate who has sold out to the machine.

Lorraine Hansberry was acutely aware of the temper of the decade in which she was writing. In the 1930s, the theatres gave expression to a popular and vital social drama in which there was no apparent conflict between the demands of drama and those of the practical idealist. The theatre of the fifties was dominated by the absurd. Social concern was at best irrelevant and at worst a symptom of man's self-destructive optimism. When Sidney rages in the second act against a world in which anger and passion have been transmuted into neurosis and unconcern, he voices the bewilderment of his age: "Yes, by all means hand me the chloroform of my passions; the sweetening of my conscience; the balm of my glands. . . . Oh blessed age! That has provided that I need never live again in the full temper of my rage. . . . Wrath has become a poisoned gastric juice in the intestine." (96)

If Lorraine Hansberry is critical of liberalism which is nothing more than naive self-expression, she is equally critical of apathy under the guise of liberal tolerance. Iris epitomises this attitude which constitutes the other side of the liberal coin. It takes Mavis to point out the implications of this moral disengagement, when Iris takes as her maxim, "Live and let live, that's all." Mavis retorts, "That's just a shoddy little way of trying to avoid responsibility in the world." (57) This desire of non-involvement is further emphasized by Iris's surname, Parodus, an implication which Mavis again underlines. Parodus, as she points out, is the Greek word for chorus, "the chorus is always there, commenting, watching . . . and being." (107)

Iris's name suggests a flower of delicacy, beauty, and femininity. Mavis's name suggests lack of imagination. Mavis was the name of a popular sweet chocolate soft drink of the time as well as the brand name of a cheap, scented talcum powder. Both of them are emblems of depressing conventionality. Gloria's name has vague religious overtones which may suggest her essential innocence.

Since hair is an ageless symbol of fertility, Iris with her long, flowing, dark hair may be considered the most sexual. Gloria, with medium-length blonde hair, appears sexual, but hers is a cold, often twisted, sexuality. Mavis's short, sculptured red hair denies sexuality, although she is the only sister with children. Iris's blue jeaned style suggests a free spirit, Mavis's simple elegant clothes reflect the control she imposes on her life, and Gloria's girl-next-door clothes reflect the person she would like to be.

Each of these women seems to feel that her life was predestined by her father. Considering her father crude and stupid, Iris thinks that she is not very bright which leads to a feeling of real insecurity. The only sister who admired her father was Mavis who sees spontaneity of a "backwoods poet" as an impossible goal. Gloria is perhaps affected most deeply. Her father called her a tramp. She became a prostitute. Even though she quits prostitution, she feels branded for life. David tells her, "Trying to live with your father's values can kill you." Gloria replies, "No, Sweetie, living *without* your father's values can kill you." (132)

Sidney's friend, Alton Scales, epitomizes black identity and pride. When Iris playfully accuses him of being a "white boy playing black boy," he replies, "I *am* a black boy. . . . I am going to make a point out of being one.' (41) Alton is an ex-communist. He talks about revolution, but he turns out to be as bound by his prejudices as the rest of the presumably emancipated characters in the play. Although he is instrumental in Sidney's first-act decision to turn political, his primary function in the play lies in his relationship with Gloria. A better scene about racial sensitivity is the one in which Iris and Sidney learn, in a letter from Gloria, that Alton has proposed to her. Their response to the news is an embarrassed silence that comes from their knowledge of Gloria's profession. That uneasy moment reveals the latent suspicion likely to lie at the heart of interracial friendship. Unfortunately the scene is effective only in retrospect, for the audience, not yet possessing the secret about Gloria, can only share Alton's doubts about Sidney and Iris.

When Alton is offended by what he takes to be prejudice on their part, Iris attacks him. He assumes that his commitment is of the same nature as Sidney's: "You and the causes all the time. It's phoney as hell! . . . The country is full of people who dropped it when they could." (40-41) Hansberry describes the substance of the speech as "Pragmatic bohemia." (41)

Lorraine Hansberry's involvement with the plight of the Negro is subsumed here in a more general concern. The human failure which is evidenced in the hardening of prejudice in racial matters is for her indicative of a more fundamental failure which underlies the capricious enthusiasm of Sidney Brustein as well as the disaffiliation of Iris. The commitment which she urges, and in which all the play's characters fail, is a devotion to humanity which goes beyond a desire for political and moral freedom. Gloria Parodus, Iris's sister, becomes the focus of Hansberry's call for compassion—a compassion which, like that identified by Albee and Miller, does not shy away from reality but rejects complacency and despair.

Gloria Parodus, like Wally O'Hara, the corrupt politician, has accepted the need for compromise—"If you want to survive you've got to swing the way the world swings!" (138) At the age of nineteen she came to the city from the country. She has become a "high fashion whore." (50) After seven years and three attempted suicides, she sees a chance to save herself. Alton Scales, Sidney's Negro friend, proposes to her and she decides to accept the proposal. When Alton discovers that she is a call girl, his own racial past combined with his physical disgust form his reaction. Gloria becomes for him a commodity which has been used by white men. In revulsion against this past, he sacrifices compassion to pride: "I don't want white man's leavings, Sidney. I could't *marry* her." (102)

Alton himself is guilty of racism when he admits that he could accept and forgive a past of prostitution, if the woman he loved were black. Their love was a casuality of the white man's oppression of the black—a history which Alton could not forgive. On the sketch she gives of Alton, Lorraine Hansberry goes back to the theme of black identity but examines it in a perspective which sees not only black assertiveness about racial dignity but also the black prejudice against the white. It is in this comprehensiveness of vision that Lorraine Hansberry's universality can be seen. When Sidney underlines the racial nature of Alton's failure, his concession is equally an admission of the fatuity of an intellectual commitment unsupported by emotional engagement: "I know it (*Touching his head*) here!" (102) His liberalism thus stands revealed as an irrelevant pose. The expansive humanity of his principles is subverted by his inability to transform it into political action. This gulf between commitment and genuine involvement rooted in passion lies at the heart of this play and also of Baldwin's *Blues for Mr. Charlie*.

The extent of this gulf is demonstrated by the fact that Gloria is failed not only by Alton but equally by Sidney, Iris, and Mavis as well. When Mavis hears of the proposed marriage, she is horrified. While aware of the therapeutic value to her sister, the idea of miscegenation seems worse to her than prostitution. Unaware that Gloria's last chance has been destroyed, she mouths the empty slogans of conservatism which seem now only slightly more obscene than those of a hypocritical liberalism: "Look, the world's not ready. . . . You have to think about children, . . . You can't expect people to change that fast." (110) When Sidney replies, it is, as Hansberry points out, "more with wonder than assertion" for he is on the edge of a new perception which does not become evident until after Gloria's death, "Mavis, the world is about to crack right down the middle. We've gotta change—or fall in the crack." (110)

Yet for all this partial enlightenment, Sidney is too wrapped up in his own disillusionment to offer any help or consolation to Gloria. Having been forced to confront the true nature of his liberalism he lapses into despair and trades absurdist aphorisms with David, his playwright neighbour, while his sister-in-law's own despair deepens into suicide. Although Hansberry feels herself at odds with some of the implications of Miller's *After the Fall,* she has Sidney mock that sense of universal guilt which Miller derived from Camus: "We are all guilty, therefore all guilt is equal. Therefore none are innocent, therefore—none are guilty." (132) This scene is reminiscent of that in which Quentin in Miller's play watches Maggie's attempted suicide. For Sidney's drunken nihilism is as surely an attempt to deny the reality of his guilt as was Quentin's refusal to accept sleeping pills from his wife's hand. Both are offered the opportunity of accepting responsibility in the act of accepting the need for compassion. In After the Fall, Quentin comes to an understanding of himself and the nature of human relationships through his experience with Maggie. Gloria's death brings Sidney to a similar understanding. This, together with his realisation of the true nature of his liberalism, constitutes that moment of "momentous enlightenment" which Albee and Miller portray. Like Quentin, Sidney comes to accept that commitment means responsibility and that freedom is circumscribed by knowledge of the ineluctable connection between action and consequence.

Sidney has a strong sense of the richness of his jewish heritage and its links to the struggle against all forms of oppression. In a key speech to Wally O'Hara, he vigorously affirms thus: "In the ancient times, the good men among my ancestors, when they heard of evil, strapped a sword to their loins and strode into the desert; and when they found it, they cut it down—or were cut down and bloodied the earth with purifying death." (96) While freely admitting that in the face of "these thousand nameless faceless vapors that are the evil of our time," he can only internalize them and then take a pill to narcotize them, he longs "to take up the sword of the Maccabees again!" (96) Thus, when Sidney is finally able to take a heroic stance and fight the evil around him, he becomes inextricably linked to the tradition of these jewish ancestors. Also, he is willing to face up to the second alternative of being cut down in a purifying death.

Sidney's jewishness, in spite of the many weaknesses he displays, enables Hansberry to express through him her admiration for the jews, historical resilience in the face of oppression and adversity, and for the sensitivity, courage, and insight that many derived from this. For all his various blind spots and waverings, Sidney is clearly a worthy descendent of the Maccabees—sensitive, concerned, and ultimately deeply committed to eliminating the injustice he sees immediately before him.

In the play, Sidney often appears to exhibit a special feeling for Alton Scales based on a close identification of jews and blacks. He fails to see his sister-in-law, Mavis Parodus, as anything other than "the Mother Middle class itself." (63) Indeed he fails to discover any positive traits in her in his righteous anger at her obvious prejudice against both blacks and Jews, especially against the blacks. Sidney plays upon her well-known prejudice by telling Mavis about a new suitor for her call-girl sister, Gloria. He does not reveal the suitor's race until Mavis is greatly excited over the prospective groom. Mavis's racism deserves such a blow. However, when Sidney introduces her to Alton, the suitor who appears to be white, and then carefully chooses the most embarrassing moment to reveal his race, is clearly portrayed as having gone too far. As Sidney makes his embarrassing revelation to Mavis, the stage directions inform us that he and Alton and Iris Brustein "variously concentrate on the food and exchange superior and rather childish glances; letting her live through the moment of discomfort." (62-63) Almost immediately afterwards, when Sidney calls Mavis "the Mother Middle class itself standing there revealed in all its towering courage" to the "snickers of delight from the diners," Hansberry's directions note that this is stated "swiftly, with open-hearted malice." (63) Mavis's response is one of the most moving speeches in the play. It is an indication of how much Sidney has overlooked her:

> I am standing here and I am thinking: how smug it is in bohemia. I was taught to believe that—(*Near tears*) creativity and great intelligence ought to make one expansive and understanding. That if ordinary people, among whom I have the sense at least to count myself, could not expect understanding from artists and—whatever it is that *you* are, Sidney—then where indeed might we look for it at all—in this quite dreadful world. (She almost starts out, but thinks of the cap) Since you have all so busily got rid of God for us. (64)

Ironically, Sidney is only "somewhat" moved "by this eloquence," whereas Alton, the target of her strongest prejudice, is "the most affected" by what she has said.

Hansberry vehemently attacks the theatre of the absurd for cutting itself off from any particular culture or cultures as well as the problems faced by individuals or groups within them for the sake of a spurious universality. Samuel Beckett's play *Waiting for Godot* takes place vaguely on "a country road" near "a tree" and his *Endgame* takes place in a room with a "bare interior . . . two small windows . . . an armchair on castors," and "two ashbins" in which an old man and woman live.[7] Similarly, Hansberry's absurdist playwright David Ragin's play is set in "a refrigerator," where two characters live who "are both male and married to each other." (58) Moreover, Sidney criticizes David for writing "fourteen plays about not caring, about the isolation of the soul of man, the alienation of the human spirit, the desolation of all love." (66) These are popular themes of absurdist playwrights. What David has really wanted to make all along is that he is "ravaged by a society that will not sanctify (his) particular sexuality!" (66) Even though Sidney makes this criticism in an appropriate context, it does seem to reflect Hansberry's considered view that the most meaningful writing deals with specific problems presented by a specific culture. Clearly, she herself pays as much attention to the multi-levelled cultural dimensions of her Greenwich village setting in *The Sign in Sidney Brustein's Window* as she did to the multi-levelled cultural dimensions of the African-American family in *A Raisin in the Sun.*

In addition to bridging ethnic and world cultures, Sidney bridges aesthetic and social concerns in a manner similar to Hansberry's. In setting up his newspaper, he pays attention to both Alton, whose bleeding heart will tolerate no concern apart from message, and Max, whose monomaniacal interest is the effect of print on the eye, never the mind or the heart. Without Sidney between them, it seems probable that Alton and Max will never be able to work on the same project. In defending the humanistic tradition in drama against David Ragin's absurdism, Sidney also expresses his admiration not only for the message that preoccupied playwrights like Ibsen and Shaw but also, more significantly, for his "stars," Euripides and Shakespeare. Wally O'Hara is a successful lawyer with a sense of humour. Furthermore, he can quote Thoreau as well as Sidney. Aware of the women 's movement, he engages in a little coterie wit: "woman's place is in the oven." (24) Sidney mistakes his glibness for sincerity and devotes himself without reservation to the campaign. After learning of Wally's deception, Sidney easily reverts to his apathetic cynical state. Wally enters making direct threats, telling Sidney to ignore the narcotics traffic and warning him that his newspaper will be destroyed. But Sidney can no longer accept corruption or the cruelties of man against man. Hansberry is endowed with a mythological sense, and perhaps saw *Sidney Brustein* as a modern-day version of the Fisher King myth. In essence, the Fisher king society of Wally is sterile and corrupt. It will prevail only as long as its members are spiritually dead. To Hansberry, spiritual decay is tantamount to lack of commitment.

With commitment comes renewal of both self and society. Hansberry thought it possible to make the water pure again. In the final scene, having been sensitized and enlarged by the complex experiences he has had in the play, Sidney can even reach out to the man who has betrayed him, Wally O'Hara, and say, "I love you—I should like to see you redeemed," although he immediately modifies this by saying, "But in the context in which we presently stand here I doubt any of this is possible." (141) The context to which he refers is the oppressive society that has "warped and distorted all of us," (141) in part by trying to eliminate ethnicity, individuality, and above all, the vitalizing variety of life that has meant so much to Sidney. This variety, the essence of a truly multi-ethnic society, is worth fighting for and is one of the things that Sidney is so staunchly ready to defend.

Lorraine Hansberry's commitment transcends the merely parochial. For her rebellion is directed less against intransigent racialism than against the sterility of the absurd and the inconsequence of a theatre founded on distraction. Like Miller and Albee, she clearly sees the dramatists' function as consisting in a compassionate statement of the need for human contact in an unattractive world. Indeed her faith in the need to face reality effectively bridges the gap between confrontation and comrnitment.

At the time Hansberry wrote, the early sixties, drugs had become a national problem reaching all levels of society. Drugs touch Sidney on a personal level that he can no longer ignore. When a seventeen-year-old employee overdoses, Sidney laments both the boy's tragedy and the continuing sale of drugs. When his sister-in-law deliberately overdoses on pills in his own home, Sidney, acutely aware of his failure to offer Gloria the assistance she so desperately needs, is compelled to take, an active stance against drugs. His decision to stand up to Wally O'Hara and the drug merchants who control him thus springs both from strong personal conviction based on bitter experience and from a desire to expiate a personal failure.

Apart from the urgent and serious ethical and social dilemmas drugs pose, it is clear that they also serve a symbolic function in the play. When his marriage is breaking down and he has just tried to sell his honour to save it, only to have his corrupt offer rejected, Sidney has an ulcer and is reluctantly induced (with ironic appropriateness) by Wally O'Hara to take a tranquillizer. As he prepares to take the pill, he proclaims to Wally: "Yes, by all means hand me the chloroform of my passions; the sweetening of my conscience, the balm of my glands. (Lifting the pills like poor Yorick's skull) Oh blessed age! That has provided that I need never live again in the full temper of my rage." (96)

The reference to Yorick in the stage directions emphasizes the role of drugs in delaying Sidney from taking meaningful and effective action. This function is further emphasized by Sidney's reference immediately afterwards to the "sword of the Maccabees" he has set aside to take the pill. The sword and the pill thereby become symbolic opponents. Gloria took pills for nearly the same reason as Sidney, to ease the emotional pain in her life. They enabled her to continue to compromise and remain a prostitute until finally they destroyed her completely. Moreover, drugs have long kept blacks and other victims of poverty and oppression from rising against their conditions. For all these reasons, when Sidney takes his stand against drugs at the play's end, he also symbolically declares that he will no longer compromise with oppression and injustice, no matter what he may have to suffer.

Despite his sporadic emotional torture, David is committed and therefore a fulfilled being who gives more than he takes. Iris and Sidney search for fulfilment, sometimes at cross purposes, and sometimes, meeting with failure. Yet the search for commitment continues, because they care. Gloria could not recognize her own power. And Max, shallow as he is, does not deserve a last name.

The Sign in Sidney Brustein's Window is a play by a Black woman writer about intellectual commitment and human dignity. It contains within itself the complex response of a very mature writer to the human condition.

Hansberry negates Absurd drama and the intellectul position behind it by giving her play a fairly clear plot, a design, and well delineated and realized characters. What she does in the play is to negate the absurdity of the world-view of her fellow Black writers who overturn the value system in their quest for a "Black aesthetic." With her firm intellectual grasp of the problem of existence, Hansberry contributes a fine play to the American dramatic tradition.

NOTES

1. Louis Gates, ed., *"Race" Writing and Difference* (Chicago: University of

Chicago Press, 1986) 67.

2. John Braine, "Foreword," "*A Raisin in the Sun* and *The Sign in Sidney Brustein's Window*" (New York: New American Library, 1966) 133.
3. Lorraine Hansberry, *The Sign in Sidney Brustein's Window: A Drama in Three Acts* (New York: Random House, 1965) 28.
4. Ellen Schiff, *From Stereotype to Metaphor: The Jew in Contemporary Drama* (Albany: State University of New York Press, 1982) 157.
5. Ellen Schiff, 156.
6. Samuel Beckett, *Waiting for Godot* (New York: Grove Press, 1978) 67.
7. Samuel Beckett, *Endgame* (London: Faber, 1958) 11.

The Collected Last Plays: A Rediscovery of African Roots

Lorraine Hansberry who died of cancer in 1965, while her second play *The Sign in Sidney Brustein's Window* was still running, left several works in progress, as well as some completed plays that had not been produced. Her last three dramas—*Les Blancs, The Drinking Gourd* and *What Use Are Flowers?*—are named under the title *Lorraine Hansberry: The Collected Last Plays.*[1]

Les Blancs is set in a mission compound—a hospital established in Africa by a European minister—and in the hut of a tribal leader. The play involves conflicting ideas during a period of change in Sub-Sahara Africa. The Blacks who once asked peacefully for freedom from the colonialists are now staging a revolution. The play focuses on three Black African brothers who reveal different attitudes towards Africa. *The Drinking Gourd* reveals the horrors and cruelties of slavery and it is, in Hansberry's own words, "a serious treatment of family relationships by a slave-owning family and their slaves." (193)

In *What Use Are Flowers?* Hansberry has an old hermit who has lived away from civilization for twenty years. He finds some wild children, who before an unnamed holocaust, were brought to the edge of the forest by someone who wanted the human race to continue. (223) The hermit sets about the uneasy task of teaching the children the rudiments of civilization.

Les Blancs offers Hansberry's most detailed and penetrating analysis of colonialism and neocolonialism in Africa. Its centrality in the Hansberry canon is to be found in that it expands the commentary begun by Joseph Asagai in *A Raisin in the Sun.* Both the structure of the play and direct statements by the major characters link the evils committed by whites against blacks to ones committed by whites against whites. This implies that neither the oppression of blacks nor their resistance to it are unique or exotic.

Most critics have noted the parallels between *Les Blancs* and *Hamlet* which deserve to be explored in detail, as they help clarify

Hansberry's view on colonialism. The parallels between the two plays help to dispel several of the misconceptions about Hansberry's intentions. The worst of it is John Simons's assertion that *Les Blancs* "does its utmost to justify the slaughter of whites by blacks."[2] This misconception is shared by a *Playboy* critic who contended that *Les Blancs* "advocated genocide of non-blacks as a solution to the race problem."[3] Viewed from the perspective of *Hamlet*, the struggle of the black protagonist, Tshembe Matoseh, against the colonial powers exploiting his country, Zatembe, is a tragic and bitter necessity, the aim of which is the ending of injustice, not the destruction of a race.

The resemblances between the main plots of *Hamlet* and *Les Blancs* are by no means casual. Both Hamlet and Tshembe Matoseh return from abroad for their father's funerals. Both are confronted by spirits who demand that they act quickly to rid their countries of grave injustices. Tshembe's spirit, unlike Hamlet's, is not that of his father, but that of a woman warrior who shares his father's values and who reminds him of the colonial power's injustices. With her urgent prompting, Tshembe recalls not only the seizure of his people's land and toil but also the ruthless cutting away of the traditional and legitimate power of his father, Abioseh Matoseh, whose position became so enfeebled that he could not openly seek redress for the rape of his wife by a white colonist, Major George Rice. The spirit then insists upon the duty Tshembe shares with his brothers, Abioseh and Eric, to be their "father's sons." (98) Further, the spirit reminds Tshembe of the underground resistance movement that his father began.

Another similarity between the plots is that both *Hamlet* and Tshembe procrastinate and take a long time to perform their duties. Meanwhile several innocent and not-so-innocent people die because the two young intellectuals have such great difficulty determining what their commitments are and how they should be performed. Like Hamlet, Tshembe is also outraged by a sexual act involving his mother. But he knows that, having been forced by Major Rice, she bore no guilt for it. She died as a result of it losing her life while giving birth to Eric. In fact, Tshembe might justifiably equate her rape with the rape of his country at the hands of European invaders.

Tshembe Matoseh, like his Danish counterpart, makes mistakes that lead to the deaths of people he cares for. He convinces a resistance leader, Ntali, to halt his attacks long enough for a respected, non-violent African leader Amos Kumalo (Jomo Kenyatta) to talk to the colonial government about a peaceful solution. But he finds that the treacherous government has put Kumalo in jail and his own treacherous brother, Abioseh, betrays Ntali to Major Rice. When he finally decides that armed resistance is the only way to end the exploitation and degradation of his people, Tshembe finds that the first person he must kill is Abioseh, a relative even closer to him than Claudius to Hamlet. However, the shot he fires at Abioseh attracts the attention of government forces outside and in the shoot-out that follows Mme. Neilsen, who matters almost as much to Tshembe as Queen Gertrude does to her possibly too-loving son, is killed.

Les Blancs, like *Hamlet*, thus ends in a bloody tragic situation that nevertheless gives the audience the impression that the condition of the country is painfully on its way to being corrected. Hansberry mixes the supernatural with the realistic in order to increase dramatic intensity and to present psychological and symbolic truths rather than to express a genuine belief in a spirit world, even though spirits were widely believed in the society the playwright depicts.

Shakespeare makes penetrating observations about honour, loyalty, passion, justice, the tragic nature of existence and so on. Likewise, Hansberry's story of a twentieth-century African Hamlet enables her to comment not only on colonialism in Africa—and, by extension, racism and exploitation throughout the modern world—but also on the exceedingly painful conflicts that sometimes arise between love and duty, the meaning and desirability of equality, and the true significance of culture and "civilization."

Hansberry's extensive use of parallels to *Hamlet* in *Les Blancs* is highly creative. First, the device permits her to pay indirect but glowing tributes to one of the finest products of English and European culture. This indicates Hansberry's keen awareness that Europe has created far more than colonialism and that much of what Europe has done remains valuable to the whole world including Africa. This appreciation is even stated explicity in the play by Tshembe: "Europe in spite of all her crimes—has been a great and glorious star in the night. Other stars shone before it—and will again with it." (125) Second, having praised the highest ideals and achievements of European Civilization, Hansberry can easily point to the number of ways in which the European colonial powers and their off-shoot, the United States, are currently failing to honour or live up to them. When Charlie Morris, an American journalist who has been seeking a dialogue with Tshembe, exposes his failure to understand the African's reference to the fierce woman spirit summoning him to fight for his people, Tshembe reminds this representative of Western culture that "when you knew her you called her Joan of Arc! Queen Esther! La Passionara! And you did know her once, you did know her! But now you call her nothing, because she is dead for you! She does not exist for you!" (81)

As Tshembe rightly implies, one of the tragic ironies of history is that many of the countries that fought battles to establish the principles of liberty, equality, and fraternity within their own boundaries have fought battles to suppress those principles in other countries solely to satisfy their lust for power. An African nationalist upholding these values may thus be judged a truer heir to the mantle of Hamlet than Europen colonizers or their American counterparts. By paralleling the European drama of *Hamlet* with the African fable of the thinking hyena, Hansberry affirms that wisdom and folly are not the exclusive property of any culture and that African culture is one of the "stars that shone before" European culture "and will again with it." (125)

Margaret Wilkerson points out that the parallels to *Hamlet* are obvious. But what is more appropriate is the invoking of the aid of an African frame of reference. "Hansberry instinctively recognizing the inappropriateness of relying only on a Western literary reference point, provides Tshembe with another metaphor—from African lore—Modingo, the wise hyena who lived between the lands of the elephants and the hyenas."[4] As Hansberry tells Patricia Marks, she agrees with those African leaders who want to take the best of what both Europe and Africa have produced "and try to create a superior civilization out of the synthesis." And her African play provides an excellent example of how such a synthesis can be achieved.[5]

In *Les Blancs*, old African myths add depth and meaning to two rites of passagedeath and initiation. When Tshembe asks Eric to tell him of their father in his last hours, Eric says, "He was just an old savage who went to his death rubbing lizard powder on his breast." (57) In African religions, the lizard symbolizes the messenger who brings the news from God that men should die. Generally the lizard was overtaken by another messenger—usually the slow chameleon—who brought news of resurrection and immortality.[6] After the Matoseh brothers paint their cheeks with yellow ochre and prepare to dance and shake bone rattles, (60) they go to the funeral ceremony, not only recognizing their father's death but celebrating his immortality.

Not only does Lorraine Hansberry use in *Les Blancs* African myths to enhance rites of passage, but she employs old folk tales to heighten the drama of the revolution. She provides a metaphor from African lore, from Modingo. In African myth, the hyena evolves from dogs and represents God's means of showing his intentions.[7] Ntali, one of the African insurgents, explains matters to Tshembe in an effort to engage him in their struggle. Modingo was asked by the hyenas, the earliest inhabitants of the jungle to settle their territorial quarrel with the elephants who demand more space because of their size. Modingo, whose name means

"One Who Thinks Carefully Before He Acts" (95) understands the arguments offered by both and refuses to join either side until he has thought over the matter. While he thinks, the hyenas wait too long. Meanwhile, the elephants move in and drive the hyenas from the jungle altogether: "That is why the hyena laughs until this day and why it is such terrible laughter: because it was such a bitter joke that was played upon them while they 'reasoned.'" (95)

In his folk tale, Ntali obviously equates the elephant with the white man occupying the land. Basically a symbol of goodness, the elephant is also associated with men and murder. The elephant therefore is both the victim and the embodiment of evil men. In Peter's tale white people in Africa are victimized by their own narrow prejudice and personify huge, selfish beasts crashing through the jungle. Hyenas, on the other hand, are sacred and holy, having evolved from dogs, which were used as a sacrifice to God.[8] The hyena which is associated with the noble black man represents God's means of showing his intentions but he also signifies God's gift to men.

At the end of the fable which Ntali unfolds in a vain attempt to enlist Tshembe in the resistance, Tshembe replies, "Ntali, the Europeans have a similar tale which concerns a prince." (95) He thus emphasizes the connection between the fable and *Hamlet*. Appropriately, among the jungle sounds that begin the play and occur frequently throughout, "the unearthly 'laughter' of a hyena is heard." (41) In this way, the figures of Modingo and Hamlet stand side by side throughout the play and are the symbolic poles unholding its structure.

Even though the tale of Modingo appears to combine the story of Kenyatta, that of Shakespeare, and a liberal dose of Hansberry, its form is unmistakably that of the African animal fable. Stage directions inform us that it "is not merely told but acted out vividly in the tradition of oral folk art." (95) This indicates that Hansberry includes the fable not only for its thematic relevance but also, more importantly, as a tribute to African artistic traditions.

By placing examples of African oral folk art, in a play based to a large extent on European drama, Hansberry suggests that in terms of thematic and aesthetic value African oral tradition competes with and blends with the European written tradition. In *Toward the Decolonization of African Literature,* Chinweizu, Onwuchekwa Jemie and Ihechukwe Madubuike argue that American oral art has been underrated by Eurocentric critics and that it has been denigrated by using tools of judgement drawn from inappropriate narrative conventions.[9] While Hansberry points out that American art and European art may not be so different in thematic and aesthetic value and parallels and blends African and European art, her juxtaposition of African religion and European-centred catholicism proves far less favourable to either culture. This is consistent with Hansberry's sceptical view of nearly all religions and her strong preference for rational humanism.

The idea that Hansberry supports is a kind of synthesis between African and European cultures, an idea later conclusively proved by James Livingstone who says "only recently have Westerners begun again to recognize the degree to which great civilizations have always been the product of mestizos. Certainly ancient Greece and Rome are prime examples, developing out of the mixture of peoples and ideas, drawing creatively from many different sources."[10]

In *Les Blancs*, primarily out of respect for his father and not because he is a believer, Tshembe prepares to take part in an African religious ceremony "to chase away the spirits of evil that have taken [his] father away." (60) To do so, he has to don "a great imposing garment of animal skins." (61) He is then confronted by his brother Abioseh dressed as a Catholic priest. According to stage directions, one is "in the mystical robes of medieval and contemporary Africa—the other in the mystical robes of medieval and contemporary Europe." (61) Later as their clash continues, Abioseh "intones a prayer in ringing liturgical Latin" while Tshembe "begins, with all his power, to join in the off-stage funeral chant." (63) At this point, the stage directions again mockingly equate African and European religions by noting that "the two barbaric religious cries play one against the other in vigorous and desperate counterpoint." (63)

In two of the most eloquent and insightful speeches in Hansberry's works, Tshembe delineates with great precision the role that race has—and has not—played in colonialism. The first of these speeches is a response to Charlie Morris's accusation that he hates all white men:

> I do not "hate" all white men—but I desperately wish that I did. It would make everything inifinitely easier! But I am afraid that, among other things, I have *seen* the slums of Liverpool and Dublin and the caves above Naples. I have *seen* Dachau and Anne Frank's attic in Amsterdam. I have *seen* too many raw-knuckled Frenchmen coming out of the Metro at dawn and too many hungry Italian children to believe that those who raided Africa for three centuries ever "loved" the white race either. (78)

In listing what he has seen, Tshembe selects examples from the major colonizing powers and demonstrates that their acts of oppression in Africa on the supposed bases of not only racial but also cultural and religious superiority are matched by domestic acts of oppression. Judged from the African viewpoint, the greatest evil of colonization may be its violation of the principle of reciprocity. According to the Ghanaian novelist, Ayi Kwei Armah, the traditional African "way" is founded on reciprocity. This principle is defined in Armah's provocative novel *Two Thousand Seasons* as follows: "Reciprocity. Not merely taking, not merely offering. Giving, but only to those from whom we receive in equal measure. Receiving but only from those to whom we give in reciprocal measure. How easy, how just, the way."[11]

In return for all that European colonial nations took, they offered only the pseudo-gifts of their own cultures and religions in the effort to control the minds of the people whose bodies they had subjected by force. They needed to convince only a handful of Africans of the value of these pseudo gifts to achieve the result they wanted. Ngugi wa Thiong'o, Kenya's leading novelist and dramatist, describes the process thus:

> The effect of the colonial presence was to create an elite who took on the tongue and adopted the style of the conquerors. They hearkened to the voice of the missionary's God, cried Hallelujah, and raised their eyes to Heaven. They derided the old gods and they too recoiled with a studied (or genuine) horror from the primitive rites of their people. The rest, for the colonial system by its very nature has room only for a few, were often deprived of their land and then herded into the settler's farms, or to urban centres to become hewers of wood and drawers of water. The first group lost contact with their roots. They despised anything that smelt of the primitive past. It is this group mostly whom Achebe must have had in mind when he cried: If I were god, I would regard as the very worse our acceptance—for whatever reason—of racial inferiority.[12]

Abioseh's acceptance of the pseudo-gifts of European culture and religion is so complete that it is obvious that he would cling to them even after the Europeans were driven from his country. This emphasizes one of the main reasons for the neocolonialism that has plagued so many nominally independent African countries. This is a neocolonialism that would put European culture, instead of African culture, in schools. It would keep African countries tied economically to the former European "masters." Hansberry, foreseeing all the dangers of this neocolonialism in its incipient stage, not only foreshadows them in the figure of Abioseh but also predicts what would eventually happen to Jomo Kenyatta and how the Kenyan government would, in Ntali's words, "trade white overseers for black!" (97) Given the enormous threat posed by neocolonialism, she recognizes that for the revolution to achieve a lasting success a dedicated radical like Tshembe will have no alternative but to kill a treacherous Eurocentric brother like Abioseh.

While permitting the wife of the Schweitzerlike Reverend Neilsen to acknowledge that "he was a good man . . . in many ways" who "did some amazing things," (125) Hansberry is ultimately harsher in her judgement of him than Gunther was of Schweitzer. Probably she views him as painfully representative of the givers of pseudo-gifts. That is, he is one of those who seek to justify unjustifiable colonialism. Idealistic and dedicated to brotherhood, Reverend Neilsen is totally incapable of reciprocity because that depends on a recognition of equals. According to Marta Gotterling, one of the doctors at Neilsen's Mission Hospital, Reverend Neilsen plays the role of Big Daddy not only to the Africans, but also to his staff. While she views this as a positive trait, the audience is forced to see it in an increasingly negative light, especially when the Reverend tells a group of Africans seeking his support for their petition for independence, "Children, children . . . my dear children. . . . Go home to your huts before you make me angry. *Independence indeed!*" (115)

The Reverend Neilsen has never been able to forgive his wife for delivering Aquah's child, Eric, or acknowledging his existence because "Eric was the living denial of everything he stood for: the testament to three centuries of rape and self-acquittal." (125) Likewise, he has never been able to acknowledge his mission's role in legitimizing exploitation and the destruction of the subject people.

Despite the overwhelming number of violations of reciprocity she depicts in *Les Blancs*, Hansberry does not preclude from consideration the possibility of true reciprocity existing between a European and an African. She includes several examples of European-African reciprocal relationships that demonstrate the attitudes and behaviour that adhere to the traditional African ethic as defined by Ayi Kwei Armah. Two of the reciprocal relationships involve Mme. Neilsen who is willing to learn from Africans as well as teach contrasts to her husband's assumptions that wisdom flows only from him and that Africans have nothing of value to teach in return. As Mme. Neilsen describes it, her relationship with Aquah is a perfect example of reciprocal education:

> Yes, Aquah. She was the dearest friend that I have had in Africa. It was she who taught me the drums and to speak the language of the Kwi people. I taught her a little English in return and a smat-

tering of French. We were just getting on to German when she died. (51)

Thus learning and teaching are also reciprocal as is Mme. Neilsen's relationship with Tshembe. Each gives and receives affection. Each has a genuine interest in the other's culture. Moreover, the two of them have almost exchanged countries so that Tshembe can remark that "it seems your mountains have become mine, Madame," and Mme. Neilsen can assert that "our country needs *warriors,* Tshembe Matoseh." (126)

Charlie, having come to Zatembe because he had a sentimental, romanticized image of Neilsen and his mission, leaves apparently committed to supporting the African struggle for liberation, because he tells Tshembe, "I've heard you." (123) Tshembe also has to be converted from liberalism to a much stronger commitment to change. Once this transformation occurs and he sees a similar transformation in Charlie, he can finally call the journalist by his first name, indicating that they now feel a reciprocal respect for each other.

Hansberry's own highly creative synthesis of forms and value from both cultures and races in *Les Blancs* makes it one of the most scathing and enduring indictments of colonialism and associated social injustices.

Hansberry's television play, *The Drinking Gourd,* is a highly charged social study of three levels of antebellum Southern society—planters, slaves, and poor whites. Robert Nemiroff observes in "A Critical Background": "Her object was not to pose black against white, to create black heroes and white villains, but to locate the sources of human behavior, of both heroism and villainy, *within* the slave society." (152)

Interestingly, *The Drinking Gourd* takes its title from a spiritual, a song of the Underground Railroad which derived, in turn, from the old slave metaphor for the Big Dipper which points to the North Star, the symbol and beacon to freedom for many an escaped slave seeking his way North in the Southern night. Songs like "Follow the Drinking Gourd" and "Steal Away to Jesus" are ingenious examples of the "signal" songs employed by the slaves to pass on secret messages and double meanings concealed in "innocent" imagery.

In the play, the links between personal choices and social conditions are evident throughout. In the Southern United States before the Civil War, the most satisfying achievement was to establish a thriving plantation. For Hiram Sweet, this success is indeed sweet and he continually recalls both to himself and to others how he started thirty-five years earlier "with four slaves and fifty dollars" and "planted the first seed [himself] and supervised [his] own baling." (181) He is proud that his hard work and ambition have paid off in the terms his society has declared to be the highest.

His son Everett too is ambitious, although a bit weaker-willed because he has grown up in the shadow of his powerful father. Everett's path to fulfilling his ambition is somewhat different from his father's as a result of his different personality and different social conditioning. His ambition is to exist exclusively as a gentleman among gentlemen "with an overseer as his instrument" (206) for directing and doing the dirty work in the fields for him. Both the market and the soil burned out by cotton required continually increased productivity to maintain the same level of profits. Maria Sweet's pride and ambition at times seem to equal those of her husband Hiram and her son Everett. But like so many women of her society, she can only fulfil her drive for power through a man.

Maria's slave counterpart, Rissa, also uses manipulation and indirection to achieve her ends although her ambitions are even more restricted and curtailed than Maria's. Having long ago abandoned all hope of gaining freedom or even a tolerable life for herself, her ambition is solely to get her son Hannibal out of the fields, where he is headed for a dangerous clash with the driver Coffin and into the house as a servant where he would not only be somewhat safer but also be better fed and better clothed. To do this Rissa has been working on the nostalgic feelings of her master Hiram. She takes advantage of every opportunity to remind him of the time when she was one of the four slaves who helped him establish the plantation. She is a strong woman who did at least as much as Hiram to make the plantation a success although she has never received a fraction of the prestige or the profits that he had gained for the labour.

Rissa's son Hannibal has a level of ambition that rivals and probably exceeds that of the man who calls himself Hannibal's master. However, his attempts to satisfy that ambition by receiving education and by preparing to escape to the North, as his brother Isaiah may have, demonstrate the dangers that face a man whose ambitions are not sanctioned by "his" society. When his desire to struggle against his exploitation and improve his knowledge of the world and his life bring him to a confrontation with Everett Sweet, Hannibal finds how cruel and absolute are the restrictions placed on his ambition. The strength of his will and his desire for freedom are then clearly shown by his readiness to try to escape from the plantation even after having been blinded. Personal will can be exerted even under the most adverse social conditions, but a very high price may be extorted for it. Hannibal is presented not simply as an individual but as a representative of a large number of slaves willing to pay any price to gain freedom.

No less than any of the others, Zeb Dudley, the poor white farmer, is a man of ambition. Ironically, however, his desire to build a plantation bigger than Hiram Sweet's leads him to become a pitiful tool of Everett Sweet. The moment Everett Sweet arrives and offers Dudley a job as overseer, he is instantly ready to abandon his project. When his first act as an overseer, whipping Hannibal for his general behaviour rather than for any specific offence, meets with Everett's disapproval, Zeb proudly asserts that "there's some things have to be left up to me if you want this here plantation run proper, Mister Sweet." (206) However, when he is later compelled to blind Hannibal, an act he finds totally abhorrent, Zeb takes refuge from his painful guilt-ridden acquiescence in the classic excuse of so many arrested Nazis, "I was just following instructions." (212) At this point, he gladly accepts the dehumanizing role as an instrument, a role which repelled him once. Ambition thus is manifestly a powerful part of human nature. It can have strongly beneficial or destructive consequences, depending on the social framework in which it is exercised.

Another aspect of human nature that takes different forms in different societies is in the roles ascribed to men and women and the concepts of manhood and womanhood that define these roles. Several concepts of manhood appear in *The Drinking Gourd*. Hiram Sweet's idea of manhood significantly involves violence, power, possession and family tradition. He tells Rissa about his most treasured possession, an old weapon he has kept in perfect condition: "My father gave me this gun and I remember feeling—I was fourteen—I remember feeling, I'm a man now. A true man. I shall go into the wilderness and not seek—my fortune—but make it!" (187) Thus, after Hiram's death, when Rissa takes the gun out of the cabinet to help her son Hannibal, a new family tradition based on mutual affection and survival is established in place of the older, more destructive one. Even more significantly, Hiram's selfish vision of manhood is symbolically replaced by Hannibal's. It entails resistance to all the dehumanizing forces of the plantation system. Before being blinded, he had intended to "come back" and buy Sarah and "Mama too, if she's still livin." (176) After his blinding, he too is preparing to go into a wilderness, as Hiram did when he was fourteen. But he will be sharing his journey with Sarah and Joshua who must do as much for him as he does for them.

The myth of womanhood is discussed thoroughly by Robert Nemiroff in "A Critical Background"—the idealized, comforting and ultimately distorted image of the Mammy. As Nemiroff explains, the image is that of "the Black Mother figure, patient, long-suffering, devoted and indomitable, heroic if need be but above all *loving*. And forgiving." (156) Rissa, who indeed possesses most of these virtues, is not inhumanly forgiving. When Hiram's son blinds and tortures her son, she neither pardons him for not preventing this cruelty nor places his welfare above that of Hannibal's. She sweeps away his defence that "some things do seem to be out of the power of my hands after all" and that "Other men's rules are a part of my life" with the bitter rejoinder, "Why? Ain't you *Marster*? How can a man be marster of some men and not at all of others." (215)

When Hiram lies dying outside her cabin she refuses to go to his aid, thus taking revenge on him for his temerity in daring to assume the role of God over her and her son. Notably, Rissa is not the only slave to turn her back on this supposedly kind master. As "he cries out for help . . . one by one the lights of the cabins go out and doors close," (215) thus turning his death into a form of collective revenge. Although Hiram is not directly involved in Hannibal's blinding and torturing, in a sense he is indirectly responsible for it. He actively supports the widespread prohibition of learning among slaves because he, like other slave owners, recognizes the dangers of education.

Sarah's love for Hannibal is strong. In spite of being the most overlooked character in the play, Sarah is noteworthy for her growth from a timid girl. She is terrified at the thought of escaping or even making the slightest gesture of defiance in front of whites. But holding her terror in check, she can seek, gun in hand, to lead a blind man and a boy to freedom with her. The reason for this growth is obviously her affection for Hannibal. At the play's beginning she is afraid of what might happen to Hannibal as a result of his recklessness in constantly challenging the authority of the driver Coffin. Sarah's full recognition of how evil slavery is, is revealed in her song "Raise a Ruckus," sung in the slave quarters far from prying whites:

> My old mistress promise me
> Mmm Mmm Mmm
> (Mimicking)
> "Say-rah! When I die I'm going to set you free!"
> Mmm Mmm Mmm
> But a dose of poison kinda helped her along
> Mmm Mmm Mmm
> And may the devil sing her funeral song!
> Sarah pantomimes gleefully helping "Mistress" along to her grave with a shoving motion of her hand. (197)

Though Sarah is afraid at first to run away with Hannibal, what changes her is her horror at the punishment Everett inflicts on Hannibal. Love makes Sarah heroic. She, Hannibal, and Joshua, for all their individual weaknesses, show a collective strength as a family that gives them hope for survival in a world dedicated to their destruction. Rissa is convinced that her other son Isaiah died while escaping, although Hannibal disputes this. She is terrified that a similar fate awaits Hannibal. When she learns that she is wrong about the possibility of gaining even minimal security in slavery, however, she unhesitantly and ruthlessly assists, and perhaps even plans, her son's and grandson's escape in the company of Sarah.

One of the major sources of conflict between Hiram and Everett is the education that Hiram provides so that Everett might acquire a social polish and an understanding of the world that Hiram lacks. As Hansberry develops it, thirst for knowledge, another highly influential aspect of human nature, is governed by a multitude of ironies in plantation society. In the case of Hiram and Everett, the irony, not restricted to the antebellum South, is one of a self-made man seeking to give his son advantages he never had and then finding that possessing the advantages makes the son despise him.

Hannibal has carefully analysed every element of slavery. He knows that his labour is being stolen from him for another's benefit. He is acutely aware of the meaning of every step he takes. He knows full well what would happen if he is discovered studying with Tommy. But he feels that literacy is worth any price. After being blinded, he still feels it is worthwhile to try to escape.

Irony abounds when, after being caught taking lessons from Tommy and knowing a hideous punishment is imminent, Hannibal taunts Zeb, "I kin read and *you* can't." (210) This statement infuriates Zeb because it establishes Hannibal's superiority in one respect which undercuts Zeb's only claim to any form of superiority—his whiteness. Hannibal's education is challenging to Everett who has constructed his self-image on the basis of his education. He bitterly resents that "a monkey-faced idiot!" can perform any part of his elite accomplishments even if on a demonstrably lower level. (209) The severity of the punishment he metes out is perhaps as much in response to his wounded ego as it is to his slave owner's fear of the effects of education on a slave.

A black cultural achievement that has attracted greater attention is that of music. Spirituals, work songs, hollers, and chants play a central role in slave culture and have laid the groundwork for jazz, blues, and rock and roll. They demonstrate some of the most striking and significant ways in which blacks continued to assert their right to call their soul their own in the midst of a society bent on soul theft and their destruction. As Hansberry states, both music and religion were often used by slaves as part of a cultural warfare against planters. This cultural warfare is highly explicit in the song, "Raise a Ruckus," which allows even persons as timid as Sarah to express aggression and anger against their "masters" and "mistresses" in the privacy of the quarters.

With this television play, Hansberry makes it extremely difficult for any American to forget or deny, as she puts it, "that their Federal Union and the defeat of the Slavocracy and the negation of slavery as an institution is an admirable fact of American life."[13]

Hansberry's response to Samuel Beckett's play *Waiting for Godot* is shown in her short play *What Use Are Flowers?* This work demonstrates her awareness of the deep chord that Beckett's vision of absurdity had struck in herself and other intellectuals of her time. Hansberry's play everywhere engages Beckett's on the most profound level, posing image against image, feeling against feeling, vision against vision. The confrontation between Beckett and Hansberry begins with their differing responses to absurdity. Beckett's image of the two tramps—Vladimir and Estragon—provides a powerful vision of futility and the absurd, especially because Godot has made only the vaguest of commitments to meet the tramps and maybe change their lives in some possibly significant way. As Esslin reports, Beckett once told an American director of *Waiting for Godot*: "If I knew [who Godot was], I would have said so in the play.[14] As Esslin has cogently argued, "such works as *Waiting for Godot* are essentially concerned with conveying their author's sense of mystery, bewilderment, and anxiety when confronted with the human condition. They reveal a sense of despair on account of an inability to find meaning in existence. In *Waiting for Godot,* the feelings of uncertainty from the hope of discovering the identity of Godot are themselves the essence of the play." (45)

Hansberry agrees with Beckett and the other absurdists that existence has no preordained meaning, that much or even most of life is uncertain, and that security is an impossibility. But she believes that humanity has the arrogance, strength and courage to do what the apes never will—*impose* the reason for life on life."[15] Accordingly, her basic response to the absence of a pre-arranged order to life or a pre-established set of values is not despair or terror, but rather assertive hope. She insists that in spite of the "thousand . . . indescribable displays of man's very real inhumanity to man," human race does command its own destiny and that destiny can eventually "embrace the stars."[16] Elements of the absurd abound in *What Use Are Flowers?* But they are matched throughout with examples of humanity's striving for mastery over nature and life itself. As Margaret Wilkerson writes, Hansberry "understood the ambiguity of the human condition: fragile yet filled with potential and possibility."[17]

The play begins in mystery and irony. An old hermit, a former English Professor, Charles Lewis Lawson, has come to a plain where he expects to find a forest and encounters several savage children who puzzle him because he expects them to act like civilized children. The mystery is eventually clarified: a nuclear war has destroyed all human life except for the Hermit and apparently this small group of children who have been left alone for quite some time. The Hermit, who turned his back on humanity twenty years earlier because of his disgust at its folly and viciousness and whose worst impressions are now fully confirmed, is shocked to find himself the sole representative of this despised civilization. He is the only person who can teach its values to the children. Everytime a child reverts to violence, the Hermit asks himself anew if his attempt to ensure the continuance not merely of the human race itself but of some basic traits of culture is the most abysmal absurdity of all.

The Hermit's most intense despair comes when his prize pupil, Charlie, has a fit of jealousy when another boy, Thomas, is praised for rediscovering the wheel shortly before his death. He even complains of being tormented in his "last absurd hours" by the children whom at the moment he regards as "unteachable." (260) His last words are significantly directed at Charlie: "the uses of flowers are infinite." (244) This is a qualified and somewhat ambiguous reaffirmation of the values the Hermit was taught. His use of the past tense signals his continuing doubts about his effect on the children and whether they have a viable future. Nevertheless, in contrast to the ending of *Waiting for Godot* in which the tramps talk about going but remain frozen in place (their immobility suggesting a permanent inability to resolve their situation), in the last action in *What Use Are Flowers?* Charlie leaves the dead Hermit and joins the crowd of children surrounding Thomas who is "patiently reconstructing" the wheel "that Charlie had broken." (261) This act simultaneously implies that Charlie has gained some understanding and self-control as a result of the Hermit's lessons and affection and that some elements of humanity will always strive to move forward despite odds.

As Esslin has noted "the subject of [Beckett's] play is waiting, the act of waiting as an essential and characteristic aspect of the human condition." (50) He notes further that Beckett views the act of waiting like the experience of absurdity itself. It is imbued with uncertainty and despair: "Waiting is to experience the action of time, which is constant change. And yet as nothing real ever happens, that change is itself an illusion. The ceaseless activity of time is self-defeating, purposeless and null and void. The more things change, the more they are the same. This is the terrible stability of the world." (52)

A further problem arising from this view of time is the damage that it does to any sense of identity. As Esslin points out: "The flow of time confronts us with the basic problem of being—the problem of the nature of the self, which, being subject to constant change in time, is in constant flux and therefore over outside our group. . . . Being subject to this process of time flowing through us and changing us in doing so, we are, at no single moment in our lives, identical with ourselves." (50-51) Hansberry too was concerned with problems of time and identity, but from a different perspective.

When the Hermit first encounters the children, he informs them that "one of the reasons" he left civllization is that he "could no longer stand the dominion of time in the lives of men and the things that they did with it and to it and, indeed, that they let it do to them." (232) However, after having ceremonially thrown away the watch, he discovers that he cannot escape the effects of time, or the desire to have at his "command again" the labels of hours and minutes that humans have created. He realizes that time exists in itself and "has a value of its own." (233) He further says that humanity has accomplished something important by coming to terms with this value. After all, the ability to record time enables human beings to record their own actions in time, to examine themselves in relation to time. Moreover, a positive attitude toward time may, to some extent, entail a positive attitude toward history, a belief that humanity's actions count for something and that progress, however slow, often disrupted and unpredictable, remains possible and desirable. Although the Hermit would steadfastly deny this view of history, his later actions and teachings imply at least a limited acceptance of it.

Hansberry presents identity as a hard-won and highly fragile achievement established through a number of incidents and decisions over a large number of years. During their initial appearance, the savage children are almost indistinguishable apart from sex and fighting strength. The Hermit's first act when he decides to teach them is to name them, "from having to remember who [they] *really* are as [they] got older." The naming is clearly the first step on the road to identity. None of the children achieves a fully developed personality by the play's end. But the children have begun a process that will lead them to a sense of identity.

In teaching them language, vocational skills, and the humanities.

the Hermit is demonstrating in miniature the agonizingly slow and difficult process of developing the most fundamental tools of civilization. The frequent interruptions of his humanizing lessons by jealousy and violence reveal how fragile these tools have been throughout history. This is especially so when one considers humanity's greatly increased potential for destruction through nuclear warfare. Nevertheless, the play's ending suggests that although the potential for total destruction may never be eliminated, humanity's drive to construct is also strong and offers at least some hope for survival.

According to the Hermit, love is one of the things that give life value, even though it may not always be pleasant or practical. Moreover, in contrast to Beckett's play, wherein the two tramps can only show the little love of which they are capable by trying to help each other commit suicide and, failing that, by helping each other wait fruitlessly for a man who never comes, the Hermit demonstrates his love by being the Godot who came for the children and who stayed with them, even through the times when they disappointed him and he disappointed himself. But, one of the Hermit's greatest virtues which strengthens his character is his ruthless analysis of his flaws.

High regard for language is clear in *What Use Are Flowers?* When the Hermit first encounters the children in their pre-lingual savage state, each is ready to tear the others apart for a scrap of food. Although they travel together, there is no sense that they have any real links among them. At the play's end, they still fight each other in envy, jealousy and spite. They still have a long way to go to build a spirit of community. But they advance in the direction of gathering to watch Thomas reconstruct the wheel that will benefit them all.

The high importance of language as an instrument for survival is evident throughout the play. The Hermit's first steps to help the children care for themselves are to give them names and to teach them the names of various objects. He soon moves on to the "abstract concept . . . 'Use'" which he regards as "vital" and one they "will have to master . . . quickly." (241) By steadily building their vocabulary and understanding, the Hermit increases his ability to teach them how to perform practical tasks such as making pots, cooking food, and building huts. A few minutes before the Hermit dies, Charlie feels the urgency to describe the tragedy which left the children alone and wild. Hands and body flowing in articulate sign language, he tells the Hermit that a huge vehicle, rolling like a stone, brought them to this plain, where great blades of grass grew high and mighty trees stood. Grasping a lily, he says, a woman brought them there. She kissed each child, went back home, and then the circle of his arms falling down the Sun collapsed.

Anguished by this recital of destruction, the Hermit declares: "Dear God: What a strange tribe they were! Lunatics and heroes all." (258)

Bereft of their parents and teacher and stripped of their humanity, these five-year olds were forced to survive in the bleakest of circumstances. They had no knowledge of building shelter, cooking food, cultivating gardens, curing illness. The prime shock of the explosion erased all capacity of speech. War in *What Use Are Flowers?* is the only villain. The children's naked bodies and frozen speech serve as grim reminders of the spoils of war.

Towards the play's end, Charlie starts using simple phrases, a newfound ability that indicates a growth in his understanding. He puts his relationship with the Hermit on a new level and enables him to develop even further by asking questions concerning matters that still puzzle him. Hansberry has thus reversed the characteristic disintegration of language of *Waiting for Godot* by presenting as vitally necessary construction of language.

Hansberry also believes in the ability of language to beautify and enrich life through literary expression. As the Hermit notes, once the children become skilled in language they feel compelled to write verses because that is the fullest form of self-expression. When the Hermit lists some of the great achievements of civilization, perhaps lost forever through the nuclear holocaust, he concludes with "the perceptions of Shakespeare and Einstein," (260) both of which exemplify the richness of language and its ability to heighten our understanding of the world and of humanity.

What Use Are Flowers? is a simple but moving reply to *Waiting for Godot.* There is a Godot who strips bare the children's savage defenses to find innate goodness, beauty and love. After twenty years of seclusion, the Hermit has discovered Emersonian "Perfect Sweetness" in the "midst of the crowd" of children, whom he imbues with humanity and independence.

The Collected Last Plays crystallize Hansberry's artistic and political philosophy of the individual and institutions, enslavement and freedom. Throughout the plays the stress is on the cold wind of deliberate action. In *Les Blancs*, Madame Neilsen describes the beginning of the revolt: "Some cold wind blew in over our people here and chilled their hearts to us." (51) The cold wind is revolution—not reform of people who have passively suffered under tyranny. The cold wind is a fitting image for less sophisticated people in warm, sensual climates. The cold wind is then the Mau Mau Revolt in *Les Blancs*, escape from the destruction of slavery in *The Drinking Gourd*, and somewhat more vaguely the atomic holocaust and the Hermit's restoration of humanity to the wild children in *What Use Are Flowers?* A devotee of Brecht, Hansberry detested senseless war, but she understood the necessity of passive resistance, direct confrontation, and at the most extreme, violence when corrupt societies repressed the vital right of the individual, that is, freedom.

Behind the vibrant theatre of the 1960s and 1970s stand the pioneering figures and themes crafted by Hansberry who forced the American stage to a new level of awareness of human relevance. In play after play, she sensed the mood of her times and anticipated the importance that African politics and styles would assume, the regeneration of commitment among American intellectuals, the equality of men and women, and the proliferation of liberation struggles throughout the world. The theatre was a working laboratory for this dramatist who reached out to a world at once cruel and beautiful.

NOTES

1. Robert Nemiroff, ed. (with Critical Background), *Lorraine Hansberry: The Collected Last Plays* (*Les Blancs, The Drinking Gourd, What Use Are Flowers?*), Introduction by Margaret B. Wilkerson, Foreword and Afterword by Julius Lester (New York: New American Library, 1983).
2. John Simons, *Uneasy Stages: A Chronicle of the New York Theatre, 1963-1973* (New York: Random House, 1975) 296.
3. "Theatre," *Playboy,* January 1971, 37. Cited in Steven R. Carter *Hansberry's Drama: Commitment amid Complexity* (Urbana and Chicago: University of Illinois Press, 1991) 102.
4. Margaret B. Wilkerson, "Introduction," in Robert Nemiroff, 18.
5. Lorraine Hansberry, Unpublished texts of an interview with Patricia Marks for Radio Station WNYC, New York, March 30, 1961. Cited in Steven R. Carter, 106.
6. John S. Mbiti, *Concepts of God in Africa* (New York: Praeger, 1970) 104-5.
7. *Ibid.*, 102.
8. *Ibid.*, 98.
9. Onwucheckwa Jemie Chinweizu, and Ihechukwe Madubuike, "African Fiction and Poetry and Their Critics," Vol. 1 of *Toward the Decolonization of African Literature* (Washington, D.C.: Harward University Press, 1983) 32, 38.
10. James T. Livingston, *Caribbean Rhythms: The Emerging English Literature of the West Indies*, ed. James T. Livingston (New York: Pocket Books, 1974) 1-14.
11. Ayi Kwei Armah, *Two Thousand Seasons* (Chicago: Third World Press,

1979) 27.
12. Ngugi wa Thiong'O, *Homecoming: Essays on African and Caribbean Literaturs, Culture and Politics* (New York: Laurence Hill, 1972) 10.
13. Robert Nemiroff, 145.
14. Martin Esslin, *The Theatre of the Absurd*, 3rd ed. (Harmondsworth: Penguin, 1987) 44.
15. Robert Nemiroff, 224.
16. *Ibid.*, 225.
17. Margaret B. Wilkerson, Unpublished texts of "The Dark Vision of Lorraine Hansberry," cited in Steven R. Carter, 143.

For Colored Girls: Quest for Black Female Identity

Ntozake Shange is known best for her "choreopoem," *For Colored Girls Who Have Considered Suicide/When the Rainbow is Enuf.* It is a moving work full of choral poetry and portraying feminine black experience. Definitively, Shange's theatre emerges from her own experiences as a poet and dancer, and she empowers her actors to experience and to communicate her dramas personally and individually.

Choreographer Dianne McIntyre, with whom Shange has both danced and collaborated on a number of theatre pieces, highlights the improvisational dimension of choreopoem: "Choreopoem is an ancient [African] form—words and movement happening simultaneously. It's natural. Zaki made a name for it. The uniqueness of the form as I know it and have worked with it, is that the words are not separate over there and danced to. The words and dance become one—intertwined so you couldn't imagine one without the other. It feels very natural to me—but it is somewhat daring. . . . Her words have the music and the dance in it and the words also have space that is open for the dance (like abstract music) whereas some other poetry may be so explicit that movement with it is redundant."[1]

Shange draws upon her personal experiences as a black woman to passionately express her concerns with racial, political and feminist issues. The seven women representing the colours of the rainbow speak of the double oppression of being black and being a woman. Shange's voice is always lyrical, whether she is recounting an episode of bleak exploitation or evoking a mood of resignation and quiet strength. She has a keen ear for black American idioms recreated in the rhythms and nuances of the language of her characters. Her choreopoem consists of chants, poetry, dance, and rituals, and recalls the salient features of African theatre.

Shange describes the choreopoem as a cycle of poems combined with music and dance. In this choreopoem, she explores the sufferings and joys of seven black American women and rejoices in their ability to share and overcome their sorrows. Critics have found fault with Shange for her unsympathetic treatment of black men who are depicted as obstacles to the social and spiritual freedom of black women. However, the play can be viewed as an affirmation of the people's will to survive. Thematically, the choreopoem moves from innocence to experience, from youth to adulthood, from ignorance to knowledge, from ignorance of self to self-knowledge, from darkness to light, from particular women's experiences to a collective black female experience and identity.

The choreopoem can be regarded as a literary coming-of-age of black womanhood in the form of a series of testimonies which in Shange's words, "explore the realities of seven different kinds of women."[2] Indeed, the choreopoem is so rich that it lends itself to multiple interpretations which vary according to one's perspective and experiences.

The choreopoem *For Colored Girls* offers a quest for new being stemming from an experience of nothingness. In Shange's poems the experience of nothingness is born of the double burden of being black and being a woman. But the stories she tells bring a shock of recognition to every woman who has given too much of herself to a man. The heart of the experience of nothingness in the choreopoem is a woman's experience of loss and debasement of self on account of the love of a man. But what makes Shange's poems more than just another version of *Lady Sings the Blues*—a theme of sorrow and survival too familiar to Black women (and white women)—is Shange's refusal to accept the Black woman's sorrow as a simple and ultimate fact of life. She probes for a new image of the Black woman that will make the old images of the coloured girls obsolete. Shange envisions Black women "born again" on the far side of nothingness with a new image of Black womanhood that will enable them to acknowledge their history while moving beyond it to "the ends of their own rainbows." The rainbow works as a metaphor for the collective voice of women of colour; it also describes the visual impact of these women moving about the stage in an array of different mono-chromatic costumes. Visually and aesthetically these women are a rainbow and only collectively are they able to dramatize the fullness of black female identity. The rainbow also symbolizes a physical beauty in the ethnicity of the black female as well as a spiritual beauty she understands when she becomes aware of her own inner rhythms.

Shange is a gifted poet/playwright who orchestrates symbols in her choreopoem *For Colored Girls*. These indices to tonal form advance meaning in Shange's choreopoems. One symbol in *For Colored Girls* that legitimizes women's vision is the array of colours worn by the seven women, including brown, yellow, red, green, purple, blue and orange. These colours of the rainbow suggest the diversity of women and limitless possibilities. Shange uses the rainbow myth presuming that a pot of gold can be found at the end of a rainbow to illustrate that these Coloured women are moving toward something good, liberating, and dynamic. Shange also uses the elusiveness and ephemeral nature of the rainbow to demonstrate the mystery of life, particularly of the lives of her women who have been marred by strangers and acquaintances alike. There is a certain amount of illusory hope expressed by these women who do not always understand why they have been victimized. With names lower-cased, suggesting self-effacement, invisibility, and a lack of self-confidence, these women battle the storm before they can enjoy the quiet of the rainbow. The unconventionality of *For Colored Girls* is evidenced in Shange's inclusion of brown and purple as colours of her rainbow. While purple may represent indigo and violet, brown is clearly a non-rainbow colour. Adding brown works effectively on a number of levels. First, brown characterizes the skin colour of black people. Secondly, brown connects these coloured girls with fundamental elements of earth, evidenced not only in the flower imagery throughout but particularly in the concluding moments of the choreopoem. And finally brown sets the prevailing mood of the piece, until the closing moment as one of gloom and despair. The dullness that is associated with brown colour is transformed into a final moment of natural colour—of sisterly communion, communion with nature, and communion of the body and spirit.

In the stage production six actresses dressed in the colours of the rainbow—yellow, red, green, purple, blue, orange—and one dressed in the brown of earth and warm-toned skin alternately speak the twenty odd-poems, each a story. While one speaks, the others listen attentively or mime the story creating a sense of sisterhood and sharing. When a story is told by one woman it often evokes sympathetic "yeahs" or the telling of a related story or even dancing from the other women. The sense of dialogue in Shange's choreopoem which raises the consciousness of woman is an invitation to the women in the audience to tell their stories. A tapestry of experiences emerges interwoven with a sense of plurality and commonality.

The title of the poem provoked questions of why Shange had to use outdated term "colored" which Black people abandoned as oppressive in the sixties. As an answer to these questions Shange explained in a television interview why she used "colored girls" in the title of her poem. She spoke of the importance of Black self-definition and of taking pride in dark skin and American heritage. Her own name

"Ntozake," is an African name which she chose as a way of affirming her African roots. But she said that it was also important to affirm her American ancestry. Recalling her grandmother's last words to her that she was a precious "little colored girl, " Shange realized that "Colored" was not only a term used by whites to define Blacks, but also a term of endearment in the Black community. The juxtaposition of "Colored girl" with "rainbow" enables Black women to see the varied tones of their skin as a reflection of the glorious hues of the rainbow, not as a colour to be borne in shame. And, though coloured girls have considered suicide because they have been abused by white society and Black men, this need no longer be the case. "The rainbow" is now understood as an image of their own beauty, and it "is enuf."

The women in Shange's play have journeyed through one emotional minefield after another, bouncing back from the blows which have been levelled at them by males. These women console each other as they speak of how they fought for integrity and self-respect. Though the evolving black women speak of the brutal treatment accorded to them by their men, Shange emphasizes their struggle to rise above this form of bondage and their success at coping with a world where "Being alive, being a woman, and being colored is a metaphysical dilemma."[3] These women have been knocked down, but they pick themselves up and search for a way to hold on to their sanity and to improve their lifestyles. In her essay, "For Colored Girl*s*—And White Girls Too," Toni Cade Bambara supports this point:

> What is curious about the work is that though men appear exclusively as instruments of pain, there is no venom, no resorting to a Queen of Hearts Solution off with his head! No god-like revenge, no god-like forgiving Hell, some things are unforgivable. The women of the various pieces suck their teeth, storm, sass and get on with the miracle of living.[4]

Shange's works dignify women's suffering and inform females that they have a responsibility to love themselves and each other enough to resist oppression. Her female characters battle with the incomprehensible dilemma of living in a world where being female and black makes them twice oppressed.

For Colored Girls is unified by a series of similar experiences shared by characters whose names are lower-cased to represent the poor, abused self-effacing women of colour. On one hand, the choreopoem speaks of the physical and emotional abuse enacted against black women. On the other, this work is about women's possibilities, their ability to survive in the face of loneliness, rejection, pain, rape and invalidation. The substance of the choreopoem is embedded in its title, says Shange, who feels that a rainbow, which comes after a storm connotes the possibility "to start all over again with the power and the beauty of ourselves."[5] According to Shange, this theatre piece is an "exploration of people's lives and provides hope for women who have known the bitterness of the storm."[6]

For Colored Girls begins with a poem spoken by the lady in brown about the importance of naming and celebrating experience in song and story:

> Sing a black girl's song
> bring her out
> to know herself
> to know you
> but sing her rhythms
> carin/struggle/hard times
> sing her song of life
> she's been dead so long
> closed in silence so long
> she doesn't know the sound
> of her own voice
> her infinite beauty. (4)

"Woman must write her self: must write about women and bring women to writing, from which they have been driven away as violently as from their bodies. . . . Woman must put herself into the text—as into the world and into history—by her own movement."[7] Helene Cixous speaks about *ecriture feminine.* In a bid to find a language like hers, women have not only adopted post-structuralist theories of language but have used sexuality and subjectivity for describing their feminist interests. In *Feminist Practice and Post-Structuralist Theory* Chris Weedon makes a case for the appropriation of recent French theories of language and culture. These theories enable women to analyse the injustices of patriarchy and women's resistance to them. Women writers and critics have keenly felt that the female experience and the creation of women characters have been falsified or distorted. In the light of these theories espousing women's cause, a plethora of texts have appeared, produced by women writers written with a strong political consciousness and awareness of recreating "real" images of women. It is in this context Shange's work presenting sexual and social pressures acquires a special accent.

Shange, in order to sing a coloured girl's song, must recreate the language of her experiences, a language which in its concrete particularity has almost never been spoken. The voices of the Black women have been negated by the standard English grammar that has forced Black people to fit their experiences into alien language patterns. Black women's experiences have also been negated by a literary tradition that celebrates the experiences of white men. Shange ignores standard grammar in her effort to capture the nuances of Black women's speech patterns and experience. The lines spoken by the lady in yellow are characteristic of Shange's style:

> it was graduation nite & i waz the only
> virgin in the crowd
> bobby mills martin jerome & sammy yates
> eddie jones & randi
> all cousins
> all the prettiest niggers in this factory
> town
> carried me out wit em
> in a deep black buick
> smellin of thunderbird & ladies in heat . . .
> all mercer county graduated the same nite cosmetology secretarial
> precollege autoshop & business
> all us movin from mama to what ever waz out there. (7)

The idiom of this Black girl's life is reflected in her speech patterns, choice of words, details of description, spelling and punctuation. The lack of punctuation and capitalization may reflect Shange's perception of the particularities of Black women's speech and experience. The lady in yellow speaks positively and unashamedly about her first sexual encounters and it renders a daring and important social break in traditional female behaviour for Shange's coloured girls. Further, it boldly announces Shange's commitment to acknowledging sexuality as a natural dimension of female identity. It renounces a traditionally reversed notion of female virginity in patriarchal societies.

Virginia Woolf once remarked that the translation of women's speech into writing would require the introduction of a new sentence. She said that women's experience does not fit neatly into the rhythms of dominant and subordinate clauses that were patterned after the ordered and hierarchical world of upperclass (white) men.[8]

In her own writing Woolf explored a stream-of-consciousness style, which, she felt, expressed women's experience more fully. Like Shange's poetic lines, Woolf's sentences lack precise beginnings and endings and patterns of subordination. In both Woolf's and Shange's writing, experience is perceived as a flow with pauses, but without the clear ordering required by the standard sentence and paragraph. Shange and Woolf would probably argue that their writing styles reflect more directly lived experience and that the order expressed by the standard sentence is an imposition, an attempt to control reality. Shange's poems also reflect her notion that Black speech is close to music, an understanding expressed in the mixed genre choreopoem in which music, dance, and spoken word are woven together.

Shange's determination to make her poems reflect female experience and bodies is evident in all the poems in *For Colored Girls*, especially in those poems that consider abortion, rape and relationships between Black women and Black men. For Shange, it is important to affirm her Black woman's body and this is reflected in many of the poems. As Shange says, "with dance I discovered my body more intimately than I had imagined possible. With the acceptance of the ethnicity of my thighs & backside, came a clearer understanding of my voice as a woman & as a poet." (xi) Through the particularities of Black woman's story, Shange touches a core of pain and self-negation shared by most women.

The first poems of *For Colored Girls* create a mood of youthful optimism, playfulness and joy in being alive. The serious note of the opening poem is interrupted by the singing of the childhood song, "mama's little baby," the reciting of a playful rhyme and a game of tag. This lighter note, which carries over into the next two poems, expresses Shange's perception that the Black girl's childhood does not always prepare her for the struggles and hard times of her adult experience. As Shange says, "*For Colored Girls* . . . is a record of me once I left my mother's house. I was raised as if everything was all right, And in fact, once I got of my house, everything was *not* all right."[9]

The poem "now I love somebody more than," tells the story of the lady in blue's teen-age fascination with the Caribbean rhythms of Puerto Rican musician, Willie Colon. Beginning with the first "Ola" (11) and moving through vivid descriptions of her dancing, " i waz twirlin hippin givin much quik feet," (12) the poem is an invocation to the spirit of music and dance that has brought so much joy to a coloured girl's life.

In white culture the Black woman's sensuality and sexuality have been viewed negatively. Black women have been viewed as sexually loose, as having animal-like passions and as willing whores. These images of the white man's imagination have been used to justify sexual abuse and rape of Black women by white men. Despite these stereotypes Shange has chosen to begin her choreopoem with a celebration of Black women's sexuality and love for music and dance. In doing so, she affirms the body and its rhythms of sensuality and sexuality and rejects those white male images of humanity that denigrate the body and sexuality.

The women of this theatre piece experience a communal yet intensely private discovery of their unique worth and strength. The first two poems celebrate Black women's life force. The next poem, "no assistance," tells of their abuse. The lady in red speaks of the many ways she tried desperately to encourage a man to love her. Instead of reciprocating, he used her only to satisfy his sexual desires. A characteristic of this Choreopoem is that the lady in red, through her acting and humour, distances herself from pain and expresses her anger and anguish at having to take responsibility to end the affair:

> this waz an experiment
> to see how selfish i cd be
> if i wd really carry on to snare a
> possible lover
> if i waz capable of debasin my self
> for the love of another
> if i cd stand not being wanted
> when i wanted to be wanted & i cannot
> so
> with no further assistance & guidance
> from you
> I am endin this affair
>
> this note is attached to a plant
> i've been waterin since the day i met
> you
> you may water it
> yr damn self. (14)

The anger expressed in her last words to this man is the anger of a woman who has realized that she doesn't need to waste her time on a man who does not value her. Her story calls up feelings of pain and outrage that such an obviously creative and funny woman has not been able to find a man to appreciate and love her.

From physical, psychological and social sufferings inflicted upon female victims of rape, the choreopoem moves to still another distinctly female suffering also related to female sexuality—abortion. Whether a pregnancy results from a consensual or coerced sexual encounter, abortion itself is a metaphoric rape that can also leave deep and lasting scars. "abortion cycle # 1" (22) details the violent procedural invasion of a female's body:

> tubes tables white washed windows
> grime from age wiped over once
> legs spread
> anxious
> eyes crawling up on me
> eyes rollin in my thighs
> metal horses gnawin my womb . . .
> & i didnt say a thing
> not a sign
> or a fast scream
> to get those eyes offa me
> get them steel rods outta me
> this hurts
> this hurts
> & nobody came (22-23)

This account of an abortion experience works imagistically on a number of levels. Images of "legs spread," "anxious," "crawling up on me," "rollin in my thighs," "tween my legs," and "gnawin my womb" recapture the action and atmosphere of both forced and consensual sexual intercourse. The language of the poem, however, clarifies this experience as one of great physical and psychological torture and discomfort. Images of blood and shattered bones reinforce not only the physical violence of the surgery itself but also the effect on a victim of sexual assault. That rape victims are often silenced by fear of their lives parallels the silent terror of this gender-specific experience.

The next two poems speak of painful violations of women's bodies in rape and hack abortion. All the women speak the rape poem together affirming that this is not an individual story. Using gang rape as a metaphor for pressing charges describes the raped woman's sense of double violation and humiliation—first by the rapist, then by the criminal justice system. A final humiliation is that friends can be rapists: Women are often "betrayed by men who know us" (19) and "we cd even have em over for dinner/ & get raped in our own houses." (21) The picture created by Shange's poem is brutal but true.[10] The stark simple lines of the poem and their harsh rhythm contrast effectively with the mood of joy expressed in the first two poems. They deepen the feelings of pain and outrage that were introduced in "no assistance." Shange creates a mood preparing the audience to experience even deeper nothingness in a Black woman's story.

In "abortion cycle # 1" Shange recreates a woman's terror during an illegal abortion. The woman sees dirt and metal instruments. The images become more brutal, the feeling of disgust grows, "metal horses gnawin my womb || dead mice fall from my mouth." (22) These images capture the feeling of violation, the pain of an abortion without anaesthesia. It was as though something huge and powerful was inside her womb, like death coming out of all her orifices. The woman explains that she sought the abortion because she wasn't married and "i cdnt have people/ lookin at me/ pregnant."(22) Her shame dissolves into pain as she cries inside, "this hurts/ this hurts me."(22) At the end of the poem her feelings of isolation and shame return as she concludes, "& nobody came/ cuz nobody knew/ once i waz pregnant & shamed of myself."(23)

In the poem about abortion the indictment is not of a male who abandons a pregnant woman. Instead, it is an indictment of a society of men and women that ostracizes women who celebrate their sexuality freely. Shange has sensitively portrayed the trauma of abortion, a trauma which, to some extent, probably exists in every case no matter how strongly a woman might advocate the right to choose abortion. Still, the black movement's rhetoric linking birth control to genocide, cannot be lightly dismissed. These considerations ought to make clear the delicate balance between blackness and womanhood which Shange manages to strike in *Colored Girls*. Maintaining this balance is no easy task. The black woman writer of some political consciousness is under tremendous pressure not to sacrifice issues of blackness to those of womanhood and vice versa.

Sechita's image of herself as an empowered Egyptian goddess is Shange's celebration of Afro-centrism and an abandoning of western ideals that particularly restrict African-American women's creative possibilities. Sechita dances in the dust of the tent of a tawdry carnival. Though she moves with an elegance that recalls "quadroon balls" (23) or Egyptian Goddesses "performin the rites," (25) her talent and beauty are not appreciated by redneck audiences. Sechita's story tells of the degradation of a Black woman's sexuality and creativity and of her defiance of those who degrade her: "they were aimin coins tween her |thighs| sechita/ egypt/ goddess/ harmony/ kicked viciously/ thru the nite/ catchin stars tween her toes." (25) She refuses to let herself be debased by the dirt and vulgarity of the man who comes to see her, envisioning herself as a Goddess and expressing her contempt with vicious kicks of her legs. Sechita's brightly-coloured costume contrasts her mood of despair as she feels degraded and belittled in a job where white men throw coins towards her genitals as she performs. Whatever the circumstances that brought Sechita to this bar, she is disillusioned and dissatisfied, believing that "god seemed to be wipin his feet in her face." (25) The traditional masculine christian God here contributes to her suffering whereas the final moments of the choreopoem move the women toward an awareness of an inner god of realized selfhood that spiritually satisfies.

The childhood reverie about Toussaint L'Ouverture shows a black female's positive fantasies about a black male who "didnt low no white man to tell him nothin." (26) The little girl, upon meeting one who alleges that he is Toussaint Jones, gives up fantasy for the reality of the boy in "those skidded out cordoroy pants/ a striped teashirt wide holes in both elbows." (29) This poem captures an important aspect of a young girl's imagination. A Black man's story is certainly more inspiring to a little coloured girl than one about big city white boys. Yet even this story teaches her to put her hopes in men as her saviour. Like Doris Lessing's Martha Quest and many other women, this little girl believes that the man standing before her is like the man of her dreams. Even though this story ends on a positive note, it shows how a little girl's fantasies prepare her for disappointments with men.

The story "One" told by lady in red is that of "the passion flower of South-west los angeles," (31) a lady in heat dressed in "orange butterflies & aqua sequins" and out to entice "every man who waznt lame white or noddin out." (31) Shange describes this woman's craft and beauty—"her stomach outlined with small iridescent feathers." (32) Despite her bravado, the passion flower really wants to be loved and appreciated. Though the lady in red describes with humour the way the mere sight of her as a "reglar colored girl" banished the lover of the night from her bed, no amount of humour can gloss over the pain this woman felt as she "cried herself to sleep." (35)

The painful irony in this poem is that this woman's power to conjure men vanishes with the water in her bathtub. Waters that purify and cleanse, so that "she became herself," (34) return her to being a sorry coloured girl. Men flee when they see her as she really is. This experience of the inadequacy of her own self and her own body is shared by all women who feel ugly and undesirable without make up and without getting dressed in the latest fashions. Black women experience this sense of inadequacy even more deeply than white women because the ideal of beauty is always white. So while Shange admires the passion flower's sense of style as expressed in her costume and even in her bath salts and respects her ability to give men a dose of their own medicine, she also recognizes that the passion flower's power is illusory until she can also be loved as she is a "regular colored girl."

In the next poem "i useta live in the world," Shange contrasts the universe of free Africa with its "waters ancient from accra/tunis/ cleansin me/feedin me," (36) with Harlem where "my ankles are coated, in grey filth/ from the puddle neath the hydrant." (36) Black women in Harlem not only live in poverty and filth but also suffer verbal and physical abuse from men. "NO MAN YA CANT GO WIT ME | I DONT EVEN| KNOW YOU | NO/I DONT WANNA KISS YOU| YOU AINT BUT 12 YRS OLD," (37) she screams. The ultimate degradation she suffers is on account of the knowledge that she must become violent if she is to survive. "i cant be nice to nobody/ nice is such a rip-off . . . is just a set-up." (38-39)

The next poem, "Pyramid," concerns three friends whose closeness is expressed as "one laugh/ one music | one flowered shawl | knotted on each neck." (39) However, they allow themselves to be split up by a man. It is an old story of women considering men more important than their friendships with each other. In this case, the women betray a close affinity with a man who doesn't even care for any of them. He conquers one, then goes after the other two who resist his advances at first and then succumb. Finally the first one finds "the rose/ she left by his pillow/ . . . on her friends desk." (41) When the two women go to confront him, they find him with yet another woman. Shange concludes the poem with the two women confronting each other:

> She held her head on her lap
> the lap of her sisters soakin up tears
> each understandin how much love
>   stood between them
> how much love between them
> love between them
> love like sisters. (42)

The poem on "between" in these lines brilliantly captures the paradox of these women's friendship. Though they allow love for a man to *come between* them, a bond created from shared experience and suffering, reasserts itself. Like Adrienne Rich, Shange celebrates the bond of sisterhood between women as a more reliable source of support than romantic fantasies about men.

In the next series of poems "no more love poems," Shange explores the experience of nothingness created by women's dependence on men. These form the introspective centrê of the choreopoem. The lady in orange sings a "requium for myself/cuz i/ have died in a real way." (43) The death she suffered was caused by self-denial and self-deception. In these lines Shange expresses an understanding of why women take abuse from men without complaining.

The lady in blue wonders whether it is worth it to be open and vulnerable if it only leads to a deeper experience of nothingness. To her the ideal of the rational man celebrated in the philosophies of white males doesn't reflect "spiritual evolution cuz its empty & godliness/ is plenty is ripe & fertile." (45) Shange rejects their denigration of the body and emotions. Her model for perfection is not the emotional and material world, but the African gods' and goddesses' expression of the life force.

In the final poem of "no more love poems," the poet confesses her inability to make her experience congruent with her philosophy. She may not be able to find a man to love her, but she can at least refuse to be a victim. The other women join her in her refusal to take abuse, asserting that their love is too "delicate," "beautiful," "sanctified," "magic," "saturday nite," "complicated," to be thrown back in their faces. Their joint affirmation has more power than the individual assertion. In celebrating their sisterhood with each other, each woman affirms her value in community. Though these coloured girls are from different geographical regions in North America and bring to the group varied personalities and varying background and experiences, they have in common their oppression which is not geographically or environmentally specific. Their being outside major cities emphasizes their social alienation from the "inside" because of gender and race. This notion of "outside" has been internalized and has become a catalyst for many of the actions in the choreopoem. Added to this, they are initially "outside" of themselves unaware of their true worth. Towards the end of the choreopoem, the women's negative and externally defined identities as black females are replaced by satisfying inner self-definitions.

At last able to affirm themselves as they are—coloured and sometimes sorry, open and in need of love—the women face a final challenge as the lady in red tells the story of Crystal and Beau Willie Brown. Beau Willie Brown's economic, psychological, and social profile reads: drug addict, paranoid, Vietnam Veteran who has returned home not as a hero, but as a pauper and drunk. He lives in a hotel room, further emphasizing his own displacement upon returning "home" after the war. He is not totally without ambition because he does try to get a job and an education. Indeed Beau Willie is not created without Shange's sympathies:

> he came home (from Vietnam) crazy as hell/ he tried to get veterans benefits/to go to school & they kept right on puttin him in/ re-

> medial classes/ he cdnt read wortha damn/ so beau/ cused the teachers of holdin him back & got himself/ a gypsy cab to drive but his cab kept breakin/ down/ & the cops was always messin with him/plus not/ gettin much bread. (55-56)

That "there waz no air" (55) in Beau Willie's life is caused in part by the capitalist system into which he was born. Consequently, he falls short of the white patriarchy's fundamenal definition of manhood. In Beau Willie's frustrated efforts to save himself, he lashes out at his only potential sources of salvation—Crystal and their own children. And in destroying them, he is suffocated by circumstances not exclusively of his own making. Although Beau Willie actually drops the children, Crystal is also responsible for what happens to her and her children. After all, it is Crystal who first brings the children into the couple's adult dispute. In a moment of bitterness and powerlessness, reacting to the unsubstantiated rumour "that Beau waz spendin alla his money/ on the bartendin bitch down at the merry-go-round cafe/," Crystal gets a court order "saying beau willie brown has no access/ to his children." (56)

Ultimately both Beau Willie and Crystal destroy their children because of their own selfishness and inability to communicate with each other. Sandra Flowers defends Shange's presentation of black men by offering an insight into the complexity of Beau Willie Brown's character:

> Beau Willie Brown is the quintessential black man of his generation (i.e. the Vietnam era). By this I do not mean, nor does Shange intend to imply that Beau Willie Brown is all there is to black manhood. Conversely, I am not suggesting that the political realities embodied in Beau Willie justify his treatment of or his attitude toward Crystal. Instead, I believe that Shange's compassion for black men surfaces most noticeably in this poem and that her characterization of Beau Willie recognizes some of the external factors which influence relationships between black men and women.[11]

At no point does Shange minimize Beau Willie's victimization. At the same time, she does not, as Staples seems to do, condone his aggressive and abusive behaviour. Moreover, Shange suggests that women like Crystal are partly responsible for their oppression at the hands of the patriarchy. For whatever reason, Crystal stays in an abusive and destructive relationship.

Crystal allows Beau to hold her child only because she is so starved for love and kindness. But Beau takes advantage of her wavering and "jumped up a laughin & a gigglin/a hootin & a hollerin/ awright bitch . . . you gonna marry me." (59) When Crystal refuses again, he kicks the screen "outta the window/& held the kids/ offa the sill" still screaming "you gonna marry me." (59-60) When Beau Willie tells her to scream her acceptance to the neighbours, Crystal "stood by beau in the window/with naomi reachin/for me/& kwame screamin mommy from the fifth/story/but i cd only whisper/& he dropped em." (60) Beau Willie Brown's dropping of his two children from a fifty-story window as a helpless Crystal looks on is an instance of male brutality. He is violent, abusive, deceptive and irresponsible. He seems to offer nothing but destruction to Crystal's life. Indeed, this example of male brutality and Shange's general presentation of males throughout the play make *For Colored Girls* more than another black feminist's ruthless attack on all black men. These images and potrayals have led critics and audiences to assert, with Robert Staples, that in "watching a performance (of for colored girls) one sees a collective appetite for black male blood."[12] Jaqueline Trescott insists that Shange's men "are scheming, lying, childish, and brutal baby-killers . . . beasts humiliated for the message of sisterly love."[13]

Shange does show that Beau Willie is a victim of a racist and capitalist society that defines manhood as the ability to be economically, physically and psychologically able to care for oneself and one's family. And while Beau Willie and Crystal wish to embrace traditional values of family and marriage they represent the antithesis of a social ideal. Almost in the same manner, Toni Morrison in *The Bluest Eye*(1970) presents a black family's reality as the complete reverse of the American ideal of family. Like Shange, Morrison offers domestic violence, both physical and verbal, as a cultural reality within black families. Both authors offer the view that violence is not something innate for blacks but may be an expression of powerlessness against the multi-layered oppressions of classism, racism, capitalism and sexism.

The lady in red finally breaks the silence with her cry, "i waz missing something." (60) Her cry reminds everyone of the loss of her children. The other women deepen her cry. The lady in blue finally names what is missing "a layin on of hands," to which the other ladies respond; "strong," "cool," "movin," "makin me whole," "sense," "pure," "all the gods comin into me/layin me open to myself." (61) Their words describe the sensations felt in a laying on of hands, an ancient healing ritual that is often practised in evangelical sects in poor white and poor Black communities. The ladies explain that a laying on of hands is not sex with a man, or a mother's comforting touch, but a touching in which powers larger than the self are channeled into the one being healed. The laying on of hands ritual affirms the self's position in a community and in the universe. It suggests to the woman that she is not alone. The laying on of hands in a community of women celebrates the power of sisterhood and sharing, as one of the keys to a woman's moving through the experience of nothingness.[14] Not only do these women acknowledge their unique position in the social and political order, but their knowledge is a declaration that they are no longer spiritually or socially dead, no longer "clothed in silence; they now hear and recognize the sounds of their own voices."

Like Chopin's Edna at the sea, Atwood's protagonist in the woods, and Lessing's Martha walking by the Thames, Shange's lady feels a connection between her rhythms of being and those of nature. The lady in red concludes, "we are the same as the sky, we are here, breathing, living creatures and we have a right to be everything."[15] The final words of the lady in red, which are picked up and sung gospel style by the other women, are an incredible affirmation of her own power of being: "i found god in myself/ and i loved her/i loved her fiercely." (63) These words express the affirmation of self of being a woman, of being Black, which is at the heart of *For Colored Girls.* The final lines express Shange's conviction that the Black woman's quest for being is grounded in the powers of being. More than just a statement of self-affirmation, this woman's finding God in herself is an acknowledgement of her self's grounding in larger powers.

In *For Colored Girls*, Shange manages to transform personal pains associated with race and gender into a public celebration of black women's potential for selfhood and self determination in a racist and sexist society. While the experiences are not necessarily autobiographical and while there is a distinct focus on black female realities, the experiences connect with a larger womanist and feminist community. While poet and playwright Amiri Baraka defined revolutionary theatre of the 1960s as "the holiness of life . . . the constant possibility of widening consciousness,"[16] Shange's colored girls find a "holiness of [themselves] released" in this revolutionary black feminist celebration.

Shange's affirmation of the God in herself is a revelation of a new way of viewing the world and of being woman. To say "i found god in myself/ and 1 loved her/i loved her fiercely" is to say in the clearest possible terms that it is all right to be a woman, that the Black woman does not have to imitate whiteness or depend on men for her power of being. This affirmation is a clear vision of new being on the far side of nothingness.

Shange adamantly rejects any traditional Christian reading of the religiosity of the final moment, insisting that

> "i found god in myself" is feminist ritual. It's feminist hedonist awakening. . . . It's hedonist in the generic sense of hedonist as feminist self-realization that allegedly occurs. . . . [The black woman] finds it [god] in herself: she does not find it [God] outside [herself].[17]

Generally we see the black woman only peripherally as the protagonist's lover, wife, mother, or in some other supporting role. Certainly black women can identify with the predicament of black men. Black women can identify, for example, with the problems articulated in Ellison's *Invisible Man* because they share the same predicaments. But for black women the predicament of the black male protagonist is compounded by concerns which effect them on yet another level. This then, is what makes *Colored Girls* an important work which ranks with Ellison's *Invisible Man,* Wright's *Native Son* and a handful of other black classics. It is an artistically successful female perspective on a long-standing issue among black people.[18]

Shange in the choreopoem does not glamorize black females at the expense of stereotyping black men. She recognizes as fact that men abuse women and that "in a crunch, [men] can always rely on their brute force" (Personal interview).[19] Clarifying her objective, Shange explains that her "target" in the choreopoem is not Black men *per se,* but the patriarchy in general which [she] view[s] as universal in its oppression of women.[20]

While her choreopoems celebrate black female identity Shange at no point encourages women to eschew all social or intimate contact with men as the solution to male exploitation. She works toward a level of communication in male-female relationship that is built upon mutual respect, trust and individual self-worth.

NOTES

1. Dianne McIntyre, personal letter, 11 June 1991.
2. Ntozake Shange, *For Colored Girls Who Have Considered Suicide/When the Rainbow is Enuf* (New York: Macmillan 1977) xii.
3. Elizabeth Brown, "Ntozake Shange" in *Afro-American Writers after 1955: Dramatists and Prose-writers,* Vol. 38 of *Dictionary Literary Biography* (Detroit, 1985) 240.

4. Toni Cade Bambara, "For Colored Girls—And White Girls Too," *Ms.* 5 (September 1976) 38.
5. Charles Moritz, ed., "Ntozake Shange," *Current Biography* (New York: The H.W. Wilson, 1978) 381.
6. Claudia Tate, *Black Women Writers at Work* (New York: Continuum, 1983) 171.
7. Helene Cixous, "The Laugh of the Medusa," *Signs* (1976) 4.
8. Virginia Woolf, *A Room of One's Own* (New York: Harcourt, Brace, Jovanowich, 1957) 79.
9. *For Colored Girls* (Original Broadway Cast recording) jacket notes, 57.
10. Herman Dianne, "The Rape Culture," Jo Freeman, ed., *Women: A Feminist Perspective* (Palo Alto: Mayfield, 1975) 41-63.
11. Sandra Hollins Flowers, "*Colored Girls*: Textbook for the Eighties," *Black American Literature Forum*, Vol. 15 (Summer 1981) 52.
12. Robert Staples, "The Myth of Black Macho: A Response to Angry Black Feminists," *Black Scholar*, Mar.-Apr. 1979, 24-33.
13. Jaqueline Trescott, "Ntozake Shange: Searching for Respect and Identity," *Washington Post*, 29 June 1976: B5.
14. Hallie Iglehart, "Unnatural Divorce of Spirituality and Politics," *Quest*, 4, 3 (Summer 1978) 20-22.
15. Ntozake Shange, *For Colored Girls* (Original Broadway Cast recording) 28, line 7.
16. Amiri Baraka|LeRoi Jones, "The Revolutionary Theatre" (1966), in *Selected Plays and Prose of Amiri Baraka|LeRoi Jones* (New York: William Morrow, 1979) 130
17. Personal interview, unpublished, August 1986.
18. Sandra Hollins Flowers, "*Colored Girls: Textbook for the Eighties*," 51.
19. Ntozake Shange "Personal interview," 10 August 1986. Cited in Neal A. Lester, "Shange's Men: *For Colored Girls*, Revisited, and Movement Beyond" *African-American Review*, Vol. 26, No. 2, 322.
20. Yvonne Smith, "Ntozake Shange: A Colored Girl Considers Success," *Essence,* Feb. 1982, 12.

Three Pieces: Quest for the African Continuum

For *Colored Girls* was followed by a trilogy entitled *Three Pieces* all of which were produced but were not successful commercially. The three plays, *Spell # 7* (1979), *A Photograph: Lovers in Motion* (1977, 79) and *Boogie Woogie Landscapes* (1979) are a response to Shange's creative encounter with the American theatre, its traditions, and its dramatic and theatrical techniques. Shange's commitment to her art is apparent when she says, "These new pieces may be non-commercial, but that's what I was and still am, as far as I'm concerned—a non-commercial artist. . . . I cannot allow myself to get trapped into a Broadway 'has been'."[1]

First of all, Shange considers herself a poet in the American theatre for whom the predominant theatrical styles have been "overwhelmingly shallow/stilted & imitative." Her interest is in "the poetry of a moment" and "the emotional & aesthetic impact of a character or a line."[2] She considers that the so-called perfect play is Eurocentric. It adopts a European framework for a European psychology. In her search for the Afro-American theatre, Shange moves in the direction of combining the blacks' pain with their art and invoking the musicals which are an integral component of black life to the aid of the theatre. That is, she attempts to move the theatre of her time into the realm of the drama of the lives of the blacks. It is in this respect that she recreates in the theatre an Afro-American language which expresses the self-conscious feelings of the community creating an Afro-American image in its essential truth. Barbara Smith in "Towards a Black Feminist Criticism" says that Zora Neale Hurston, Margaret Walker, Toni Morrison, and Alice Walker use a "specifically black female language to express their own and their characters' thoughts,"[3] but she fails to describe or provide examples of this unique language. We have recently come to acknowledge that "many of our habits of language usage are sex-derived, sex-associated, and/or sex-distinctive," and that "the ways in which men and women internalize and manipulate language" are undeniably sex-related.[4]

In the creation of a distinct Afro-American theatre, Shange points out that she has made use of what Frantz Fanon called "Combat breath." Although Fanon refers here to Francophone colonies, combat breathing is a living response to a cultural crisis. The three pieces in the collection *Three Pieces* reveal the pain and sensation experienced by Shange's characters who express their creative response to the constrictions of their humanity in the context of combat breathing. In analyzing Francophone African colonies, the social psychiatrist has argued thus:

> There is no occupation of territory, on the one hand, and independence of persons on the other. It is the country as a whole, its history, its daily pulsation that are contested, disfigured in the hope of final destruction. Under this condition, the individual's breathing is an observed, an occupied breathing. It is a combat breathing.[5]

Implicit in Shange's reference to Fanon is the understanding that struggle for liberation involves the entire community. Liberation for women necessitates a re-definition of the position of men.

For Shange, Fanon's additional characterization of combat breath involves the drive to reconcile the irreconcilable. This shows that Shange, like Fanon, often fuses concrete reality with metaphoric projections which reveal her awareness of the social determinants and her commitment to change. Sandra Richards examines Shange's world from an African world-view and points out that one of the most outstanding features of her dramaturgy is "a dialectic between the felt constrictions of the social order and the perceived limitlessness of the natural order. On the one hand, there is an awareness of social oppression and commitment to struggle; on the other there is a desire to transcend or bypass, through music and dance, the limitations of social and human existence."[6]

Shange's plays also reveal that the individual protagonists not only show combat breath but also seek to transcend corporal existence in order to merge with natural cosmic forces. According to Sandra Richards, the new world African religions such as *Voudoun, Santeria,* and *Candomble* provide a useful paradigm for the spiritual axis found in Shange's plays. Common to all these religions is the belief that the world is a dynamic interplay of forces like language, music and dance which are potent modes of the manipulation of more profound insights. American theatre has not only been influenced by European models but by non-European ones as well. It has been affected in varying degrees by Japanese Noh and Kubuki plays, Chinese Ching Hsi drama, Indian Sanskrit drama and traditional African drama, all of which contain elements of mime, dancing, stylized gestures, song, and instrumental music.[7] An examination of the plays of Pulitzer prize winning Wole Soyinka reveals that plays by contemporary African-American women strikingly resemble Africa's methexic drama, containing songs, drums, dance, rituals, masks, chants, music and the call and response. The epistemology of experience within an African world view is inseparably cognitive and intuitive. Shange's protagonists are African people raised within a Western perspective. Their Western heritage teaches them to reckon experience as fragmented rather than as holistic. Hence there is the dialectic of combat breath versus the will to divinity in the plays of Shange.

For Benston, European drama, which is basically mimetic—an imitation or representation of an action—amounts to "the spectacle observed," whereas African-American drama grows out of rituals that dissolve "traditional divisions between actor and spectator, between self and other."[8] Alvin Goldfarb and Edwin Wilson note that "while Western theatre and drama have emphasized separation of audience and actor, individual creativity, and a set text from which little variation is permitted, African theatre has emphasized audience participation, group activity, and improvisation. The result is that while the purpose of the European theatre is to entertain and to teach, that of the African is to embody and affect, and to be."[9]

Spell # 7, the first piece in the volume *Three Pieces* was originally published in 1979 by Joseph Papp's New York Shakespeare Festival in New York City. Set in a bar, it centres round nine characters, Lou, Alec, Dehlia, Eli, Bettina, Lily, Natalie, Ross and Maxine. The characters live in a country which tries to deny the blacks the right to exist. Hence they consider it a deceitful country. They discuss how the blacks are oppressed by racism in America. They also examine the plight of the black artist. They express their inability to find satisfactory jobs because the whites demand that blacks live according to their stereotyped view which presents them as inferior to them.

Spell # 7 is generally about the socially prescribed limitations of being black, particularly the problems of being a black artist. While sexism is always an issue in Shange's work as a feminist, attention to sexism and/gender roles might seem secondary to race in the piece. Racism and white America's associations of blackness with negativity, ugliness and shame are centrally focused in this piece.

Spell # 7 is not so much about individual or personal identity as about accepting the realities of being black collectively in modern America. This second published play offers no optimistic resolution to perceived and internalized problems of being black. Less abstract in terms of character and action and less idealistic, *Spell # 7* offers a poignant statement about the inescapability of racial and gender stereotypes. It also demonstrates the need for individual fantasy as a tool for survival in a bigoted society and shows the definitive need for racially segregated experience to dispel oppressive and often internalized myths about black culture and celebrates positive aspects of black identity. Instead of finding an inner rainbow after sufferings as the women in *For Colored Girls,* the characters in *Spell # 7* acknowledge a potentially futile and often hostile reality of on and off-stage role-playing.

Spell # 7 is about blacks learning to love themselves and each other. The magician casts a spell on a group telling them they are going to love being Coloured. Of this powerful piece, Don Nelson of the *New York Daily News* wrote thus: "Ntozake Shange's *Spell # 7* . . . is a celebration of blackness, the joy and pride along with the horror of it. It is a shout, a cry, a bitter laugh, a sneer. It is an extremely fine theater piece."[10]

Shange incorporates a minstrel show as the prologue to *Spell # 7* and has a large minstrel mask suspended above the stage, creating visual reminders of the play's theme of black misrepresentation and self-deception.

Shange's characters in *Spell # 7*, like the persona in Paul Laurence Dunbar's "We Wear the Mask," reveal that they have had to lie and hide the truths about their lives in order to survive in America. With the mask looming, the play opens with a magician who promises to cast a spell on black America. As if to counter all that the mask has done to shape blacks' attitudes about themselves and each other, the magician announces that he is going to make them love being coloured.

One major difference between Shange's minstrel show and traditional shows is that Shange's black minstrels do not effect stereotypical comic relief through their portrayals. They rather recall the pain of black people's history of subservience to whites.

When the magician casts his spell, the characters tear off their blackface masks, representing their freedom to reveal secrets, fantasies, nightmares and hope. They become uninhibited and begin to tell truths about the journey of blacks in America. The magician then commands the hideous, gigantic mask to disappear. Though the mask rises, it is never hidden from the view of the audience. Shange does not want the audience to forget that the mask is symbolic of oppression. She makes this clear by linking the raising of the mask to the preceding lynch mob scene. The menacing shouts, cries, and laughter of the mob cement the cast to the floor while the unmasking frees them.

Dancing is also symbolic in Shange's *Spell # 7*. Shange uses dancing and music to suggest linkages. She believes that black playwrights should not be allowed to work without dancers and musicians because "black people have some music and movement in their lives." (X) Shange links her characters by having them engage in a series of steps or dance routines that identify every period of African-American entertainment, including acrobats, comedians, tap-dancers, calindy dancers, Cotton Club Choruses and Apollo Theater duwop groups. The characters' friendships are tested and strengthened in the play as they re-enact, through dancing, the various stories of their lives and the lives of a host of black heroes, including Muhammad Ali, Ishmael Reed, Marcus Garvey, the Commodores, Bob Marley, Stevie Wonder and the Miracles. Through dancing, the characters develop a sense of familiarity and family, a shared cultural heritage. Dancing becomes a cultural communion, with the participants deriving sense of impenetrable solidarity. In an interview Shange was asked to tell about the impact of dance on her creative life and writing process. She said: "Writing is for most people a cerebral activity. For me it is a very rhythmic and viseral experience. Dance clears my mind of verbal images and allows me to understand the planet the way I imagine atomic particles experience space. I am not bogged down with the implications of language. I am only involved in the implications of movement which later on, when I do start to write, become manifest in the rhythms of my poetry.[11]

Like Childress and Hansberry, Shange levels an indictment against the American stage which mirrors ideas tainted by racism. Under the watchful eye of the hovering mask, the characters voice thier anger at the stereotypical roles that are offered to them. They express contempt at being forced to squabble over such degrading roles as mammy, prostitute, and buffoon. Bettina, a struggling actress, says "if that director asks me to play it any blacker/i'm gonna have to do it in a mammy dress." (14) Trying to comfort Lily, a fellow actress who complains that the only roles she can find are ones that call for blacks to sing and dance or shuffle, grin, hum, and pray, Bettina says, "at least yr not playin a whore/if some other woman comes in here & tells me she's playing a whore/i think i might kill her." (23) The scarcity of realistic dramatic role for blacks has been a serious concern for Shange and for countless other artists particularly because the stereotyping continues both on and off the American stage.

Shange claims that black women are unloved, unwanted and unattended because of these myths. Lou, one of the black male characters, says, "nobody loves the black woman like they love farrah fawcett—majors, the whole world dont turn out for a dead black woman like they did for marilyn monroe." (36) In another scene, a black man recently back from Europe sets in awe of a black woman who reads Nietzsche, speaks several foreign languages, and talks about global issues. The man tells her several times that she is not like any black woman he has ever met. Shange argues that this is one of the lies that racist America has fed to black men. Her message is that there are millions of black women who are intellectuals and that black women for too long have been assigned restricting labels.

If there is any question that Shange views sexism as an outgrowth of racism, one needs only examine the scene that pokes fun at white women who accept and promote these myths about blacks. Shange ridicules white women by depicting them as gullible, frivolous, artificial, and emotionally weak. Natalie, a not too successful performer, announces that she is going to be a white girl for a day. She tells the cast that the first thing a white girl does when she wakes up in the morning is to give thanks that she is not black. Shange depicts white women as paranoid of blacks, thinking that black men plot to beat, rape, murder or marry them. Also coming under attack are whites who write about blacks. The persona says, "after all, gertrude stein wanted to know abt the black women/alice adams wrote *thinking abt billie/* joyce carol oates has three different black characters all with the same name/i guess cuz we are underdeveloped individuals or cuz we are all the same." (48) Through the process of fantasizing, Natalie realizes the fullness of her own existence as a black female. Natalie's conclusion is Shange's message in *Spell # 7*, to take pride in being black. For being black means "laughin . . . lovin'. . . [and] . . . livin"—honest and instinctive emotional responses to being active. According to Shange, it also means acknowledging psychological pains that do not have to muffle out spiritual vibrance of black identity.

Shange is clearly resentful in her treatment of the white female liberal. Natalie points out that there are some white women who castigate themselves because they were not born black. Natalie says, "yes i'm sorry they were born niggahs. But then if i cant punish myself to death for being white/i certainly cant in good conscience keep waiting for the cleaning lady." (49) Shange's most severe indictment against white female liberals is her denouncement of them as women who have to take twenty Valium a day to contend with their ignorance of the world, ERA and men.

One of the characters in the play is a magician named Lou. Lou's deliberately racist identification of white people as "crackers"—perhaps the closest black counterpart to whites' use of "nigger"—diminishes white people and their attitudes toward black. And having demonstrated black legitimacy on the stage through fantasy and dream or "black magic," Lou shows blackness as a source of pride rather than shame. Both *Spell # 7* and *Boogie Woogie Landscapes* introduce elements of magic in typical Afro-American fashion. Lou casts a spell on the group when he says, "i'm fixin you up good/fixin you up good and colored/ & you gonna be colored all yr life/ . . . colored & love it/love it/ bein colored." (8) The implication here is that whites are born free but blacks have to struggle for the right to be alive. There is the portrayal of the persistence, determination of the blacks in *Spell # 7*. Blacks here demonstrate a refusal to be annihilated. The play is a celebration of blackness—the joy and pride as also the horror of it. *Spell # 7* perhaps is not a play in the traditional sense of the term. But in touching upon the many facets of black life, Shange vividly recreates a sense of powerful drama inherent in her poetic vocabulary. Her nine characters offer a conglomeration of experiences of other blacks by assuming roles of characters who do not actually appear on the stage. One of the features of Shange's characterization is that her characters appear in flashes. They give the audience a glimpse of their pain, frustration, disillusionment, loneliness and rage. Motivation of character and adequate dramatic development are absent in these plays. The idea that blacks must strive to accept and to love themselves is no doubt positive. Yet the Sue-Jean story told by Alec and Natalie deals with a character who neither warns nor can give love. Sue- Jean's desire for a baby, her pretension that she enjoyed his love-making, her masturbation and laughter at him when he left, her slitting the child's wrist when he began to grow away from her suggest implications which are not developed in the play. The story perhaps suggests that a man is needed for no more than propagation.

In the play, the minstrel performers move through the pain of dance steps and memories associated with Black entertainment. In doing so, they banish the hideous mask along with their stage personae, thereby creating a safe space in which to expose secret hopes, fears, or dreams. But two confessions come at the end of each act. The first involves a young woman who gives birth to a boy named Myself. Sue-Jean is ordinary, a "colored girl with no claims to anything/ or any one." (28) As a Black person she is defined by her poverty and low status and as a woman by her availability as a sexual object. In choosing pregnancy, Sue-Jean refuses to see herself as inert or inconsequential. She creates instead an active, engaged self. She pursues the traditional female modes of self-expression in planting a garden, canning, baking and knitting: "Sue-Jean waz a gay & gracious woman/ . . . she waz someone she had never known/ she waz herself with child/ & she waz a wonderful bulbous thing." (30) And she strives to ensure that her baby will be safe from "all that his mama/ waz prey to." (29) An "ordinary colored girl" (28) with neither satisfying social nor personal identity nor social attachments, Sue-Jean desires an identity as power over her environment. Her longing for control in her life is imaged specifically and importantly in her intense desire to bear a son.

> She had always wanted a baby/never a family/never a man/
> She had always wanted a baby/who wd suckle & sleep
> a baby boy who wd wet/ & cry/& smile suckle & sleep. (28)

Sue-Jean's life and story break with tradition in its unconventional dream of motherhood without a husband and without a father for the child. The baby's infantile dependence on her physically is what she considers most fulfilling about motherhood.

But when Myself begins to crawl and explore the world, when the male Myself, an embodiment of Sue-Jean's own self, grows into new realms, Sue-Jean kills the child and drinks his blood. She then returns to a state of pregnancy. But then it is an imagined pregnancy in which the anticipation of an impending birth is gradually superceded by the joyous feeling of being pregnant "& she forgot abt the child bein born/& waz heavy & full all her life/with 'myself.'" (32) Thus, for Sue-Jean, psychic paralysis or the liminality of being forever on the verge of self-expression is preferable.

In Sue-Jean, Ntozake Shange creates a figure whom the critic, Barbara Christian, identifies as the contrary Black woman.[12] Because she is seen as abnormal, as the "other" essentially apart from whites and Black men, the Black woman has limited alternatives. In fashioning the character of Sue-Jean, Shange embraces the concept of the nurturing female with vehemence. In killing her child Myself, Sue-Jean makes actual the suicide which many women symbolically experience in sublimating their own identities to those of their children. Sue-Jean kills her child because she is unable to exact total dependence from or exert absolute control over another and sucks his blood in a final attempt to incorporate the child into herself. She is left psychologically traumatized and paralyzed by the incident. Madness becomes an ultimate tragedy for Sue-Jean, whose portrait serves to distinguish creative fantasy from unproductive dreaming.

Shange, like early black women playwrights Angelina Grimke and Myrtle Smith Livingston, apparently feels that black and brown babies must be protected from those forces that would torture them. Sue-Jean's protectiveness is apparent when she says, "I gotta prayer cloth for the boy/myself waz gonna be safe from all that his mama/waz prey to." (29) Mentally deranged, Sue-Jean prefers to murder her child rather than see him victimized in an oppressive American Society.

Maxine is another Shange character whose actions in the final segment of *Spell # 7* seem like a contrary, ludicrous response to the sociometaphysical ills she would cure. As a young girl she lived in a house where "trees that grew into my room had to be cut back once a year/ this waz when the birds sometimes flew thru the halls of the house as if the ceilings were sky & i/simply another winged creature." (49-50) Nor did they notice that this intelligent little Black girl celebrated phenomena like polio epidemics as evidence of divine protection because "if god had made colored people susceptible to polio/then we wd be on the pictures & the television with the white children, i knew only white folks cd get that particular disease." (50)

When she becomes a young woman, however, her grandmother closes up the windows. Together with her mother, they send her out into the world to be among "trouble" but not get into "trouble." Her loss of innocence is not confined to the personal realm of the mysterious "trouble" young men present. Maxine learns that, contrary to her cherished childhood beliefs, Black people are not immune to the diseases and perversions manifested by whites. Her faith shattered, she buys gold, knowing that more than likely it comes from apartheid South Africa "to remind the black people that it cost a lot for us to be here/our value/can be known instinctively/ . . . 1 buy gold/ & weep. i weep as i fix the chains round my neck/my wrists/my ankles. i weep cuz all my childhood ceremonies for the ghost-slaves have been in vain. . . . no one understands that surviving the impossible is sposed to accentuate the positive aspects of a people." (51)

What gives arresting uniqueness to the familiar themes of the loss of innocence and the repression of natural instincts, inflicted upon young females, is the element of contrariness. Maxine's purchasing of gold is the adult counterpart to the childhood ritual of paying homage to unknown ancestors. The visible evidence of African subjugation, these pieces of jewellery are chains binding Maxine directly to the enslavers. Thus, like Sue-Jean, Maxine chooses a liminal state in which her childhood faith has been almost completely destroyed and no adult strategies have been devised to resolve the crisis effectively.

Despite the public, political implications of contrariness, one may wonder how these pictures of wounded, stagnating women are an indication of Shange's combat breath. For an answer, one must examine the thrust which Shange's playwriting assumes. Most often she does not write plays in which a crisis is resolved within the structure of the play. Nowhere is this thrust beyond the theatre clearer than in *Spell # 7*. This play attempts to create a liberated stage space for Black self-expression. Because Sue-Jean's and Maxine's confessions threaten to reveal a pain almost beyond cure, the magician/master of ceremonies must halt the action in order to reassure his audience that it takes up the refrain "bein colored & love it." With the magician's defiant reaffirmation of the right of Blacks to exist as they choose to define themselves, the minstrel mask returns, and the audience leaves.

Shange draws upon two distinct traditions in contemporary Western theatre. In her commitment to combat breath, she achieves some of the effects described in Bertolt Brecht's dramatic theories. Chief among the German dramatist's tenets is the view that the theatre must be an analytical forum which exposes bourgeois illusions and stimulates audiences to think objectively about the causes of social and personal ills. By constructing most of her plays as a series of poetic monologues, occasionally interrupted by conventional dialogue, Shange takes advantage of the poetry to encourage her audiences to listen with close, critical attention. However, the episodic structure diminishes the audiences' empathetic tendencies by denying them the opportunity to gain a more rounded sense of character. But *Spell # 7* forces both performers and audiences to acknowledge the terrible distortions of their lives.

Shange seems indebted to the French theorist Antonin Artaud, and the Black nationalist, Amiri Baraka, whose 1964 essay, "The Revolutionary Theatre," is derivative of Artaud's *The Theatre and Its Double.* In this tradition, the theatre is a place for emotionally charged, eruptive forces which assault social complacency. It exposes victims who, nevertheless, contain within themselves seeds of their own regression. But while Shange's mode of playwriting shares similarities with Artaud's and Baraka's theoretical writings, Sandra Richards would contend that her style is actually rooted in an even older philosophical tradition, that of the African world view.

Because this perspective posits the universe as animated by the interplay of energy-fields or forces, power resides not only in men and machines, but also in props, costumes, lighting and sets. All have the capacity to assert a *presence* akin to what we associate with actors/ characters. Music and dance are particularly strong in their power to convey layers of sensate information lying beyond or outside linguistic dimensions. They function as *mojos.* As spirit-forces, they have the power to amplify, contradict, or reaffirm the spoken word. As structures, they act as channels for enlightenment. In Shange's drawing upon this Black aesthetic lies the will to divinity, an impulse which her characters experience as an opposition to combat breath, as Sandra Richards says in her article "Conflicting Impulses in the plays of Ntozake Shange."[13]

Two examples of the will to divinity occur near the ends of her plays. Both follow moments shocking in their level of self-inflicted violence. Both raise issues which extend beyond the plays. The transition from "a nite with beau willie brown" to "a laying on of hands" in *For Colored Girls* and the shift from Maxine's adult method of atonement to the cast's refrain "bein colored & love it" in *Spell # 7* are the examples. In the first play, Crystal's story about the death of her children caps a long list of grievances against men. The other women have nothing to match Beau Willie's self-hatred and psychosis. For many women a performance becomes a quasi-religious event in which the hurt of personal and group relations is subsumed by the recognition that their lives are being given public validation for the first time. They experience a communal yet intensely private discovery of their own worth.

Spell # 7 is not without elements of hope. Shange challenges blacks to rise above injustices and particularly to avoid hurting each other. Natalie says, "surviving the impossible is sposed to accentuate the positive aspects of a people." (51) The play ends as it began, with the magician casting a spell to make blacks love themselves. In order not to imply that the struggle is over, Shange has the huge minstrel mask lowered while the cast sings "colored & love it." (52)

The second in the trilogy, *Three Pieces,* is *A Photograph: Lovers in Motion. A Photograph: Still Life with Shadows/ A Photograph: A Study of Cruelty* which was produced at the Public Theatre in December 1977 and revised as *A Photograph: Lovers in Motion* for Houston's Equinox Theatre in November 1979. In this theatre piece, Shange explores the notion that a person's identity is not defined by things but by a belief in self. Shange's play *A Photograph: Lovers in Motion* explores the ambiguities of male-female sexual identity. Using photograph as a metaphor for life, Shange presents black men and women entangled in a web of destructive romance. This play moves further from Shange's earlier mood of celebration to one of tense uncertainty in heterosexual relationships. Shange presents individuals working towards defining and endeavouring to resolve conflicts between their own sexual and social selves.

A Photograph has a fascinating theatrical quality about it. Its five "intertwined characters push and shove into each other's lives, making their overtures and rejections and pleas for love with seductive jestures and violent outbursts."[14] Ann Holmes of the Houston Chronicle makes a special mention of the logical progression of action and dialogue in the play and admits that the play reveals detectable growth in at least one character, that is, Sean David who is a struggling novice photographer involved with a complex triad of women. Nevada, an attorney, wishes to take Sean out of the ghetto and provide him with material comfort. Claire, a model, is a cocaine addict and a nymphomaniac who wants to possess Sean. Michael, whom Sean chooses in the end, is a dancer who wants to help Sean fulfil his dreams. Earl, another character who is also an attorney, is a homosexual who has designs on Sean. As an extension of the choreopoem technique, *a photograph* incorporates Shange's characteristic use of music, dance and poetry. It is dramatically effective to have the dream sequences of Michael and Sean as well as the characters' soliloquies in poetry. Such moments present a complexity of the characters when they are most spontaneous, emotional, and psychologically revealing. Their confusion and uncertainties about their own personal past and present are simultaneously immediate and distant as they struggle to satisfy various needs and desires. *A Photograph* is more visually oriented than either *For Colored Girls* or *Spell # 7* since characters are continually physically interacting with each other—battling or embracing.

It is not altogether accurate to treat black plays as an imitation of either European or African models. An examination of Childress' *Wedding Band* and *Wine in the Wilderness,* Hansberry's *A Raisin in the Sun*, and Shange's *A Photograph: Lovers in Motion* reveals a unique brand of theatre in which many heritages come together. The dramatic action in these plays is inextricably linked to and is defined by the experiences of African-Americans which are rooted in African rituals. Female characters in these plays journey through several stages of psychological growth. Parallels can be drawn between these stages of growth and the progression through the phases of exposition, exemplification, and resolution. The progression is undeniably linked to African- American struggle for survival and wholeness. The female characters undergo a personal and sometimes political odyssey or search for wholeness as they progress through six stages: Koinonia, logus, metanoia, kerygma, didache and eucharistia.[15]

These stages of growth, which have their equivalence in Freytag's Pyramid, are terms based on Koine Greek, the marketplace or common man's Greek spoken during the Hellenistic through Roman periods. These words lend themselves to broad interpretations and are placed in the context of African-American initiation and survival rituals. Koinonia means fellowship, a fellowship that helps to define and positively affirm a person's sense of self. The next stage logus serves to bring on confusion and doubt. This is when a black person realizes that his poverty or illiteracy or exclusion from or failure in a given field is a direct result of racism. The metanoia, the third stage of growth, involves a turning away or turning around, a quest to understand and be saved from confusion and disappointment. It marks a struggle to cope with the oppression accompanied by a series of trials and errors. The Kerygma follows the metanoia. This stage of growth centres round the heroine's compulsion to speak. Kerygma suggests explosion, sometimes verbal but sometimes physical. The message, or didache, serves as a catalyst for those who sit in judgement and catapult the heroine into the final stage of growth. The eucharistia, the final stage, is a combining of inner wholeness with outward community. This wholeness or completeness leads the heroine to cement a family that has been torn apart, whether it is a consanguineous or spiritual one. Often the heroine rejoins her immediate family, or lover, or significant other, or community to celebrate her renewed faith in the value of solidarity.

Michael does embark on a journey that results in her wholeness. She is a dancer who is in love with the struggling photographer, Sean. She is culturally and spiritually grounded. Michael's first stage of growth, Koinonia or beginnings, is evidenced as she shares with Sean the strength of her ancestors. Michael tells Sean that her people—grand parents and uncles—took care of themselves and fought for every breath every day of their lives. Sean attempts to deflate Michael's sense of self by telling her that black people are not as courageous as she imagines because he only knows of "welfare/the white folks/heroin & whores." (80) At this time Michael describes a vulnerable but resilient grandmother who carried a shotgun to protect her offspring from racists and who sat on the porch telling stories about Marcus Garvey, W.E.B. Dubois, Jack Johnson, and "the colored horse soldiers." (80)

Michael not only has the strength of her grandparents to rely upon but the stories of black heroes who offer hope to young blacks as they journey through life in America. She reminds Sean that her history is one filled with "alla the blood & the fields & the satchels dragging in the dust." (81) Shange connects Michael to her immediate and distant forbears who represent tradition, shared experiences, and the community spirit of survival. Michael shares with Sean an incident that traumatized her and shaped the lives of her entire family. She painfully recalls for Sean the details of her grandfather's savage lynching in the Carolinas. She tells him that it was at that point in her grandmother's life that she started carrying a shotgun to ensure that no more of her children would be brutally murdered by a white mob that had no respect for black life. Michael connects her own nigger moment to what she perceives as Sean's. She berates Sean for allowing Nevada to dehumanize him. Sean allows the jealous Nevada to destroy several of his photographs that serve to boost his career. Michael tells Sean that she is disappointed that he thinks that "being a nigger is being nothing." (80) She is repulsed by the fact that he allows Nevada to buy him with her money and tells him that she did not come from people who tolerated being treated like niggers.

The action of the play is advanced as Michael moves into the third stage of growth, the metanoia. At this juncture, Michael informs Sean that she wants to end the relationship involving his sexual association not only with her but with Nevada and Claire. She comes to the realization that she must turn away from Sean in order to keep her own dignity intact. This awakening is prompted by a visit from Nevada who offers to help Sean get a show at a museum. Though Sean turns down Nevada's invitation to help him, he does accept a very expensive lens for his camera from her. Michael decides that she no longer can tolerate Sean's manipulation of women and his self-debasement. Recognizing that he is a parasite and a coward, she tells him "I'm leaving . . . it'll keep me loving myself." (83-84)

Michael journeys into the fourth stage of growth when she and Sean argue about his lack of self-confidence. She tries to tell him that he is capable of great things as an artist. But that it is his fear of failings that prevents him from putting his photographs on exhibit. Sean's defence mechanism is to shout obscenities at Michael. He accuses her of not knowing anything about him, except that he is perpetually making love to her "never get enuf ass." (84) Michael is hurt by Sean's verbal blows to her self-esteem. His sense of inadequacy is infectious and Michael begins to question her own worth. However, when Sean asserts that Michael is a "stupid bitch" who can be appeased like all females, by sexual pleasure, Michael goes into a fit of rage. She regains her own sense of self-worth as she slays the dragons that plague Sean: insecurity and indecisiveness. She retaliates by saying, "i dont like thinking that you think yr dick means more to me than yr work." (86) Michael tells Sean that he is not a man, somebody who loves in the world. She mirrors for him his own emptiness and callousness.

Michael shows her love for Sean by refusing to give up on him, in spite of the fact that he abuses her emotionally. She does not stop chipping away at Sean's layers of insecurities until she teaches him he must learn to love his art, regardless of whether the Washington critics or anybody else tells him that his photographs are without quality. Though Sean grabs her and wrestles with her to silence her, she continues to spread the news to him telling him "when you work on yr pictures like you worked on me/i'll believe you/right now i think yr fulla shit & i'm ashamed cuz I believed you at least loved photography." (87) Michael prepares to leave but Sean regresses to his boyhood, during which his father loved a pet monkey more than he did Sean. Shange portrays two people who are missing something that only the other can supply: a love that satiates. Michael's growth is inextricably linked to Sean's.

Michael's reaching out to Sean not only heals the wounds left by his father's abuse but cements her relationship with Sean. Michael stands by Sean. She reaches out to him and convinces him of his self-worth. He chooses her, discarding Nevada and Claire, because she believes in him and forces him to risk sharing his work with the public. This re-joining of two lovers points to Michael's eucharistia. It is characterized by her celebration dance. As the play closes, Sean tells Michael, for the first time, that he loves her. Her response is to dance which suggests the joy and peace she has found in her relationship with a black man with whom now reciprocity, understanding and tenderness are possible.

Ntozake Shange's works often focus on the lives of musicians, dancers, visual and performing artists and so on. Her use of poetry, dance, music and choreographed lighting is her way of bringing to the American theatre the heart and soul of African-American traditions. Blacks have traditionally turned to singing and dancing because those areas were open to blacks in white America. Shange's dramatic structure is innovative, and in *A Photograph: Lovers in Motion* the poet/ playwright merges traditional dramatic structure with identifiable African-American self-expression.

Sean David is one of Shange's most confused characters. We witness his complex social, physical, and psychological responses particularly through his treatment of three female lovers. At a glance, Sean might seem the stereotypical male whose self-image is determined by his sexual prowess. He boasts of his ability to juggle several female lovers while retaining complete control over each. Yet Shange undercuts his empty confidence by showing that Sean cannot keep his women apart any more than he can separate the suffering depicted in his Vietnam photographs.

Ntozake Shange's poemplay *For Colored Girls* and *A Photograph: Lovers in Motion* are replete with chauvinists. Like Beau Willie Brown, Sean is also a male supremacist. Shange's middle-class chauvinists are no less brutal than the grassroots black men who violate their women. Sean, in this play, explains to Michael, his favourite lover, "there are a number of women in my life/who i plan to keep in my life/ & i'll never let any of them come between us/between what we have in our world." (61) During an argument, however, over Sean's lack of confidence in himself and his work, Michael tries to tell him that she knows he is capable of great things. Viewing Michael's encouragement as an attempt at emasculation, Sean tells her that she does not know anything about him except that he takes care of her sexual needs. Becoming abusive when she dares to tell him not to confuse her sex with genuine love,

Sean raves, "yr really outta yr mind/stupid bitch/i know how to deal with you/or any other bitch comes in here." (85)

Sean is equally disrespectful and vulgar to Claire and Nevada. To him, Claire is solely a mindless sex object. When Claire jokingly intimates that she may share with some other man some of rhinestones and palm leaves and magnolia, Sean's ego is bruised. He retaliates by telling her that if he ever finds out that she has gone to bed with another man, he will take her to the 500 club and "give everybody some of that magnolia." (65) That Sean could threaten to participate in the rape of his paramour illustrates his regard for womanhood.

Nevada, a lawyer, also falls victim to Sean's verbal abuse. Nevada's contradictory behaviour reveals her vulnerabilities, her extreme loneliness caused by an image of "miss society" (102) that she feels compelled to maintain. Nevada's profession as an attorney—one which requires sound reasoning faculties—offers a contrast to the irrationality and complexity of her emotional state. While she admits on a rational level that "no. i dont need nothin else. i gotta office/i gotta porsche/i gotta family & a name," (90-91) she has not convinced herself that she does not need Sean. She acknowledges her loneliness and her craving for sincere love: "& i never had nothing for myself/just this stupidness/running around being important/bein highfaluting/all this time pushing for what isnt ever gonna be mine/i do / i do/need somebody." (90-91) Although Nevada has what most would define as success—material possessions and social status she has no sense of her own identity apart from what her family's money and name can obtain. Nevada and Claire, despite their different personal and professional backgrounds, share this emotional void. Since Sean is only interested in Nevada's money and connections, he has little patience with her when she exhibits jealous behaviour. At one point when she tells him that she loves him, he responds apathetically and non-committally and orders her to get out of his sight. Sean's chauvinism toward women is also expressed by his friend, Earl, who tells Nevada that she deserves someone better than Sean who only knows women and cruelty. The key thread that joins these three women is that Sean seems to feel that each one in her own way is trying to deprive him of his manhood.

As the "stud" whose overwhelming masculinity precludes a monogamous relationship with any female, Sean is emotionally callous in his treatment of his lovers and a bisexual male friend. In an effort to validate his manhood he taunts Michael: "dont be getting all holy & above possession/aint a bitch in the world cant get jealous & loud/ they been running me crazy." (69) Such a comment reveals Sean's contempt for women. Yet in his failed efforts to arouse Michael, he becomes indignant. In direct contrast to an arrogant Nevada and a lustful Claire is Michael, who represents for Shange—and in light of the play's ending, for Sean as well—a kind of "middle ground" image of women. Michael neither bribes Sean for his affections nor allows him to exploit her sexually. Seemingly perceptive, self-assured, and disciplined, Michael often becomes Shange's mouthpiece, provoking Sean to reassess his commitment to photography and to reevaluate his views on manhood and manliness. As a friend to Sean, Michael respects his work and his person and tries to convince Sean that his is not above needing, giving, and receiving a love that simultaneously includes and transcends physicality.

Sean seems to take great pleasure in his abuse of the women who do almost anything for him—from posing nude under a shower of Jack Daniels, to parading naked with feathers vaginally inserted, to providing money for his rent and expensive camera equipment. This abuse also manifests itself in a violent temper and brute force. Using Michael as her mouthpiece, Shange works toward redefining manhood in a way that makes both females and males more whole individuals:

Michael: i thot you were a man
Sean: i fuck you fool/you still don't know i'ma man?
Michael: i mean somebody who loves in the world/ loves himself & his work & some people. (87)

To change his attitude toward women, Sean examines his sexual identity. In the painful process of self-discovery, Sean elicits our sympathies.

First, we witness Sean's examination of his literary idol, Alexandre Dumas, who defined success as materialism and manhood as sexual promiscuity. Until Sean can become commercially successful, he considers himself a nobody. His harem of female lovers temporarily satiates this obsession with *becoming* the world's greatest photographer rather than *being* a photographer satisfied with his own work. Needing to prove himself to white society and to his own father, Sean like Beau Willie is a man trapped. In the final soliloquy of Act I, he abandons his preconceived notion of manhood as granting immunity to emotional pain:

When you get to be a man/you can go to
the whorehouse
with me/that's what he usedta say
tho he brought the whores home/& fucked
em & beat em & fought em & laughed all

nite long . . .
When you can swim like me/he said/
you'll be a man
& stuck me in the water with my diapers on.
at dinner time daddy waz asleep/head
on the table
& bottle nearby . . .

my daddy didn't like me/daddy didn't like me he usedta say/mama
neither but it dont matter cuz I'm not theirs no how/i'ma man i am
a man
& he wd cry & drink his vodka/with
the lady whose name
i cdnt know/cuz i waz running the hallways
looking for a daddy. (88-89)

Sean's hostility toward his lovers is his way of lashing out at the man who was never a father to him. But the father's problems are as deeply rooted as Sean's. He too defined manhood as violence and indiscriminate sexual activity. Sean's boyhood memories reveal a father who had little respect for women, a father who "brought . . . whores home/ & fucked em//& beat em & fought em & laughed all nite long." (88)

Sean's behaviour with Michael, Nevada, and Claire parallels his father's degradation of women. The same paternal neglect has crossed at least two generations, distorting the men's perceptions of manhood. The independence thrust upon Dumas's son and on Sean does not diminish the son's needing paternal approval. Thus, each son must prove his legitimacy to another male. In a white patriarchy, the black male, in his failure to measure up to the standards of manhood set by white men, defines his manhood in terms of his ability to dominate black women. But even physical and psychological power over women does not satisfy these men's emotional and spiritual voids. In the stories of these men and their unresolved relationships with their fathers, Shange redefines manhood as gentleness, emotional vulnerability and sensitivity. These are the very qualities stereotypically and negatively attributed to women.

Sean's hostility subsides when he admits his need for real love, not just sex—which is precisely what Shange's colored girls discover and long for. Like Beau Willie, Sean David is not an abusive black man without redeeming qualities. Edith Oliver, in a review of *A Photograph*, recognizes his dilemma:

> Sean, whose camera represents his manhood and his means of attaining fame—a Nobel Prize for photography is what he has in mind—is haunted by a dreadful childhood by Alexandre Dumas, (the father and son) (who were themselves part black), and their literary and sexual achievements in nineteenth century Paris, and by some dead soldiers he photographed on a hillside in Vietnam. For all his savagery to his women he cannot be dismissed as just a male chauvinist; . . . he appears to be as much a victim of his out-of-hand ambition and his bitter frustration as (the female characters) are.[16]

What moves Sean away from the stereotypical black man is his ability to admit to himself that he is in pain and has been misguided in his move toward knowing who and what he is. Although he eventually admits that he needs to love and be loved, this commitment is rather ambiguous, given the fact that there appears to be no real change in his attitude toward the women characters even after this soul-searching.

His final relationship with Michael even takes on the stereotyped role of man as woman's protector. Perhaps Shange suggests in this ambiguity the difficulty in individual's efforts to rid themselves of socially prescribed gender roles. Yet what is ultimately significant in this play is Shange's willingness to probe beneath the surface to arrive at what causes Sean to behave as he does.

"a photograph is like a fingerprint/ it stays & stays forever/we cd have something forever/just how we want it give me a camera," boasts the aspiring photographer Sean, u & i cd get you anything you wanted/breeze/a wad of money/madness/women on back porches kneading bread/ stars falling/ice cream & drunks & forever/i cd give you forever in a night sky/michael/i cd give you love/pure & full/in a photograph. . . ." (77) Sean's unspoken assertion here is that the objects of desire and excess, from money to ice cream, from madness to intoxication, from breeze to eternity, are unrealizable on a stage lying outside the realm of the camera, outside the world of the picture. The world of Sean's Photographic construction in Shange's play is represented thus: 'i've got it all there in that frame, i gotta whole dynamic of centuries/ in a two-dimensional plane." (76) We need to listen to the photographer Sean to appreciate how the modern love affair with the camera can turn unformulated desires into phantasms of creative potency "i gotta world i'm making in my image/i got something for a change/ lil sean david who never got over on nothing but bitches/ is building a world in his image." (79) The photographic process allows Sean to objectify the world around him and to arrange the world according "to a point of view which endows it with a recognizable meaning."[17] To Sean, most significantly, this imagistic constancy provides the frame for the objectification of his own masculine self. Such an object-building through the genius of mechanical reproduction allows Sean, as Jean-Francois Lyotard puts it, "to arrive easily at the consciousness of his own identity as well as the approval he thereby receives from others—since such structures of images and sequences constitute a communication code among all of them."[18] As Sean puts it "i'm a genius for unravelling the mysteries of the darker races." (76-77)

Yet Shange does not permit Sean to receive easy approval from his interlocutors. Although his female counterpart, Michael, has little difficulty acknowledging Sean's desire to conceive the world as a picture, she does not let him forget that his self-esteem as a maker of both pictures and women is always mediated on the stage of the world by the presence of a technological character, the camera. "You tell em straight out" She taunts Sean, "that you are/osiris returned & yr camera has been the missing organ in our forsaken land." (93) As Michael dismissively interprets Sean's phallic antidote for the diseased condition of black American culture, hope lies less in the subjective impotency of its voyeuristic user than in the idealized character of the camera.

This ideological formation of camera as phallic voyeur and shaper of the female "look," serving male desire, also surfaces in *a photograph* when Sean recounts how he has made pictures ever "since we cd hide neath mary susan's window in the projects & watch her undress." (95) In these instances, the fixating camera and the desirous *male* gaze come together in a performance of masculine entrapment. Feminist critics with a psycho-analytical bias relate the theme of the male gaze on the female body in poetry & poetic drama to phallic activity and the desire for sadistic mastery of the object. For Michael, Sean's best photographs are not the pornographic ones that he knows will be commercially successful but the ones that reveal truth about the human condition, the ones revealing suffering and realities unadorned. Unlike Nevada, Claire, and Earl, Michael does not criticize Sean's dreams or his talents as an artist. Instead, she encourages him to explore possibilities of his artistry. She implores Sean to seek satisfaction with himself as a photographer, not allowing an outside world to dictate his feelings about himself as a person or as an artist.

Shange's play provides us with a striking example of a mixture of dramatic and filmic vision. The play opens with the disjunctive performances of two "struggling artists." Sean struggles to control the female subjects of his photographic art. Michael turns to her inner world of dance and movement as a fluid expression of the psycho-economic struggle: "our lives/ our grandparents & their uncles/it's how we came to be/ by taking our lives seriously/we fight for every breath every god-damn day." (80)

Michael's dances of rebellion, both inside and outside, for and against the hegemony characteristic of the age of the world picture, are what establish the conceptual framework of Shange's play. The dance is something Sean "cant have or return to/somethin dim in memory/barely articulated." (77) Always present among these lovers in motion, dance takes on the character of a cinematic memory. And while Sean displays slides of the Muslim woman whose toiletry he secretly films from across the street, Michael describes her dance to Sean, as if reinforcing the memory in its most vulnerable state:

> i am space & winds
> like a soft rain or a torrent of dust/
>   i can move
> be free in time/a moment is mine always
> i am not like a flower at all
> tho i can bloom & be a wisp of sunlight
> i'm a rustling of dead leaves
> collections of ol women by the weddin
> the legs of a cotton club queen
> & so familiar with tears
> alla this is mine/so long as i breathe/
>   i'm gonna dance
> for all of us/everybody dead/everybody busy everybody too burdened to jump thru a nite a hot & bluesy jump in the guts of ourselves a dance is like a dream/i can always remember make it come again . . . i can make it come again. (77)

The coalition of photo and dance—the fusion of technology's representations and drama's human forms—produce a screen of artistic struggle in which the crucial activity is less human agency that its representatives, that is to say, its framings, its readings, its interpretations. Responding to Sean's claim that "i thot art waz survival," Michael insists thus: "no. it's love it's fighting to give something/it's giving yrself to someone/ who loves you . . . lettin everybody in & giving up what is most treasured." (85) As Shange's visionary of moving dreams, Michael confirms that her art is framed in pathos, in struggle, in vulnerable openness. The clash of Shange's filmic bodies thus provokes us to acknowledge, to read, the structural anxieties and abstract relations enslaving art in the age of the white against black, even male against female, world picture.

Ntozake Shange taking the lead from Hansberry, seems preoccupied with broadening the American theatre to include African rituals. Shange's theatre pieces generally do not conform to traditional dramatic structure, making it difficult to detect a noticeable progression of action or character. Addressing the issue of dramatic structure in Shange's pieces, Sandra L. Richards asserts, "By constructing most of her plays as a series of poetic monologues occasionally interrupted by conventional dialogue, she takes advantage of the telegraphic, elusive quality of poetry to encourage audiences to listen with close critical attention."[19]

Shange's redefinition of what constitutes theatre in America has caused a great deal of controversy, particularly since her verse drama is antithetical to that of such established writers as Maxwell Anderson, Robert Lowell and James Scheville. Wilkerson notes that "Shange is critical of the artistic constraints imposed by the professional theatre on black writers and performers."[20] C.W.E. Bigsby points out that Shange views the originality of her dramatic form as "a necessary gesture of revolt of models of drama which she saw as alien to her own situation.[21]

Last in the trilogy is *Boogie Woogie Landscapes*, which is Shange's most experimental dramatic piece. Shange's title announces the subject of the choreopoem and the manner in which it unfolds. "Boogie woogie," a style of jazz piano playing characterized by a steady rhythmic and melodic pattern, describes both the musical atmosphere of the piece and the piece itself as a kind of improvised jazz accompaniment.[22] It blends surrealism and expressionism to form a fantasy world in which Layla and the other nightlife companions sing, dance, and share emotional ramifications of being black and female in America. Produced at the Terrace Theatre of the Kennedy Centre in June 1980, this piece suggests that it is not good to be born a girl when females are infibulated, excised, clitorectomized and are still afraid of molesters and rapists. Speaking of the play, Anne Welsh of *The Washington Star* writes, "Shange is a major poet, born in and out of theatre."[23]

In *Boogie Woogie Landscapes*, Shange experiments extensively with expressionistic techniques. More complex than *for colored girls* theatrically, *boogie* dissects the psyche of black "all American colored girl." Using characters that enter and exit through walls of the set, Shange creates a dream play where a black female's conscious and subconscious desires are visibly personified. While resembling *for colored girls* most in content and subject matter, this play moves deeper into a black female's psychological identity. That the play is structured as a dream is central to both the play's meaning and structure. As in a photograph, this play does not resolve racial and sexual tensions set forth but dramatizes the complexities within and oppressed mind. Issues of racial and sexual identity reveal that Layla, the central character, exists as a product of her immediate environment, *boogie* is an in-depth character analysis and Shange's foremost effort to define and legitimize a black female's ever-threatening realities.

As a result of the popularization of the matriarchy myth, unyielding, religious women who rob their sons of manhood appear in much of the literature written by blacks and whites. Mapp suggests that "the thin line between black mammy and black matriarch may be distinguished largely by whether the old girl is presiding over a white or black household."[24] Regardless of her moral and physical strength, though, she traditionally has been "relegated to her place in the kitchen or pantry."[25] When no other job was open to the black mother, she could find work in the kitchens of White Americans. Alice Childress, once a maid herself, contends that the black mother's function has been to serve as a maid of the world. In her article "The Negro Woman in American Literature," Childress asserts that "facing the world alone makes a woman strong. The emancipated Negro Woman of America did the only thing she could do. She earned a pittance by washing, ironing, cooking and cleaning, and picking cotton."[26] In response to the myth that the black mother has unmanned black males, Childress says that the black woman has "helped her man, and if she often stood in the front line, it was to shield him from a mob of men organized and dedicated to bring about his total destruction."[27] Using expressionist techniques, impressionistic imagery and her characteristic collage of dance, music, and poetry, Shange presents a choreopoem that is more complicated structurally, more theatrically complex and less idealistic philosophically.

Many multidimensional images of the black mother appear in literature written by black women. Mary Helen Washington asserts that the black mother is depicted as fiercely provocative of her children, often sacrificing herself to prepare them to live in a violent and racist world."[28] In her essay "Black Women Playwrights: *They Speak: Who Listens?*" Barbara Molette contends that black women dramatists have traditionally written positive images of black motherhood and tried to promote mores that were humanistic.[29] In keeping with the traditional stereotypes, many of the mothers in plays by Childress, Hansberry and Shange are selfless, determined, and saintly. They symbolize sincerity depth, strength and vitality. There are two black mother characters that escape the narrow confines of stereotyping: Lorraine Hansberry's Rissa in *The Drinking Gourd* and the nameless mother in Shange's *Boogie Woogie Landscapes*. Lorraine Hansberry apparently believed that not all slaves were content and chose to portray a black mother whose devotion to her family and whose simple, motherly act of vengeance set her apart from the archetypal black mother figure.

Another atypical mother appears in *Boogie Woogie Landscapes*. While there is not a great deal said about this mother, she deserves to be examined because she is more vulnerable, confused and disorganized, than any other mother figure to appear in literature by blacks of the period. The mother in Shange's theatre piece is a professional woman who cannot cope with the pressures of a career and a family. She is very intolerant of her children's mischievousness and even less patient with the steady flow of maids who come into her home to keep the family intact. In spite of domestic help, "the house got crazy. mama tryin to feed nine people & make lunches for five/put each one of us at a different bus stop. cuz a integration/none of us went to the neighbourhood school."/ (131) The mother gives in to her temptation to leave behind the madhouse of a home. She turns over the responsibility of the family to her physician husband, leaving the family without any assurance that she is ever coming back. By the time the mother does return the children, husband, and maid agree to be supportive of the modern-day, high-powered, and heart-attack-prone career mother.

Like the works of Childress and Hansberry, Ntozake Shange's writing reveals a preoccupation with blacks as an integral part of the African Continuum. Shange's own connectedness to Africa is evident in her name change. Shange insists that her background shaped her view of the interconnectedness of African-Americans and other people of colour:

> My parents have always been especially involved in all kinds of Third World culture. . . . I was always aware that there were different kinds of black people all over the world because my father had friends from virtually all of the colonized French-, Spanish-, and English-speaking countries. So I knew I wasn't on this planet by myself. I had some connection with other people.[30]

The family in Shange's *Boogie Woogie Landscapes* is one not frequently seen in literature. First it is an augmented middle-class black family as opposed to the grass-roots black family that graces the stage so often. Second, the images of middle-class blacks in this family are positive, including the image of the black father. The husband, a physician, and his wife, a career woman, earn enough money to afford a luxurious two-storey home and to provide for a series of live-in domestics who are perpetually plagued and provoked by the children and then terminated. These maids/nannies may be considered as part of the family because they do have a great deal of influence over the children, including teaching them manners, values and practical skills such as how to manage a home.

Though primarily an augmented one, the family shifts to an augmented, extended, attenuated family because the mother, anxiety- and stress-ridden, abandons the husband and children. The mother, depicted as puritanical, hypersensitive, and color- and class-conscious, does not like her "common" children. The young girl recalls her mother saying "I always pick the most niggerish people in the world to make my friends & then she wd list mavis & freddie & charlenetta & linda susan (who waz really po white trash) so I didnt say nothin." (134) Overwhelmed and unhappy, the mother abandons the family. In the absence of the mother, the father who is gentle, patient and loving, cares for his children with the help of the grandmother and a house keeper. The persona says of her father, "daddy brushed our braids to a point like a dunce's cap & then patted them down. He gave us way too much money for lunch & tol Grandma she waz overworkin her heart so he wd have to get someone to come in til mama figured out whether she waz comin back." (132) Shange chips away at the myth that black fathers do not take responsibility for their children. Billingsley's findings lend credibility to Shange's portrait of this middle-class black father:

> Social workers have known for a long time that there is nothing like a good steady job with adequate and dependable income to make a man get married, stay married, remain with his family, and support it, while the absence of such economic viability is highly correlated with the refusal of men to ensure the stability of their families.[31]

On another level, Shange connects this middle-class black family to its larger family, one that is not as fortunate and does include the masses of disadvantaged blacks. One of the characters, who serves as a voice of African-Americans, criticizes the *New York Times* for its shallowness and ineffectuality at treating the concerns of coloured peoples of the world. She speaks of other papers that serve as a forum and a medium in the linking of all black people. She says she will not read the *New York Times* again until it acknowledges the existence of blacks and begins to print news of merit, such as the following:

> EXTRA EXTRA READ ALL ABOUT IT:
> ZIMBABWE CELEBRATES FIFTY YEARS OF
> INDEPENDENCE . . .

> EXTRA EXTRA READ ALL ABOUT IT:
> WHITE SOUTH AFRICANS DENIED ENTRY TO
> THE UNITED STATES
> AS WAR CRIMINALS
> EXTRA EXTRA READ ALL ABOUT IT:
> NOT ONE AFRO-AMERICAN CHILD WHO CANT
> READ & WRITE/
> CELEBRATION OF CAMPAIGN AGAINST
> NATIONAL ILLITERACY. (125-26)

Shange's images of the black family are powerful and diverse .

Much of *Boogie Woogie Landscapes* deals with Layla's difficulties during adolescence. The biographical parallels between Layla and Ntozake Shange are apparent. *Boogie Woogie Landscape*s, with no traditional plot or theme, resembles the stream-of-consciousness style of James Joyce. Bits and pieces of Layla's experiences, memories, and dreams are presented in such fragmented fashion that it is difficult for audiences to find a theme in the piece.

Layla's encounter with her would-be lover stereotypes men in matters of romance—that men want only sex from women and that men will use any manipulation toward that end, an issue raised in Act II of *Spell # 7*—the scene introduces and acknowledges the inevitable paradox in male-female sexual relationships, a paradox affecting primarily women: while acknowledging her sexuality as a positive force it is shown that sexuality inevitably makes each woman vulnerable to the potential, physical, social and gender liabilities. The man, in contrast, experiences only the pleasures of the sex act, retaining physical, psychological, and social power. In fact, a male's sexuality is rarely a liability of any sort and is more often perceived as a form of social empowerment. Just as Layla learns that being black means being oppressed, she discovers that being female also means being denied certain freedoms of existence. Layla hopelessly admits that she "feel [s] like an oven" (115) recalling the oven|cave description of her home environment. Oven imagery is particularly effective dramatically and metaphorically as it reiterates Layla's emptiness and her need to be filled with something to justify her existence and worth. On still another level, oven imagery recalls a myth that explained to black children that their skin is the darker than white children's because they were "baked longer." Hence, the darker a black person's skin tone, the longer that person had been "in the oven.

Shange uses mirror imagery and speaks simultaneously of the "full regalia" of ourselves as well as "our own sweat" to suggest the complexity of any character study that treats an individual's self-reflective mental activities and physical and emotional ramifications of those activities. An image of sweating announces both the terror and the passion of Layla's existence and experiences.

n.l.C # 5
She threw herself on her bed & her sobs
roused her so/she began to beat the walls
her fists matted the surface with grime|
she turned to the doors|rubbin her face
across the thresholds|she created ebony blurs
that she cdnt even reach less she leave a furrow
of slate fingerprints|she made things black

n.l.C # 6
indistinguishable....................
....
she didnt want anything as black as the palms of her hands to touch her

n.l.C # 1
she waz black enuf awready|. (115)

Layla's inability to understand her existence in this environment produces self-alienation. Such details as her violently beating the walls with her fists and rubbing her face against thresholds graphically depict her psychological struggle and physical self-endangerment. Since the nature of dreams in Boogie is such that they are unpredictable and seemingly disordered and nonsensical but can be interpreted, ordered, and related to the real world as well as to the unconscious, Shange plays the role of an analyst monitoring aspects of Layla's psyche, some of which even Layla is unaware of. To bring order to those observations, Shange demands that her audience also become Layla's analyst. Although much of the night's dreams highhights the victimization of females politically, socially and sexually, Layla's dreams are not all nightmares. Indeed, there are instances in Layla's life, both as a child and as an adult, when she celebrates life and her identity. Layla is a black woman who overcomes her dual victimization through dance and recollections of happier times.

There is little question that *boogie* is as much about Shange as is *For Colored Girls*. She admits *Boogie Woogie Landscapes* "is the secrets and traumas of an Afro-American childhood, a *double entendre* about myself, the many different places I have lived, and their varying psychological topography,"[32] and adds: "in boogie . . . i presented myself with the problem of having my person|body, voice & language| address the space as if i were a band|a dance company & a theater group all at once cuz a poet she do that|create an emotional environment| felt architecture."[33] *Boogie Woogie Landscapes* is then another song of the inner rhythms of black female existence. Yet Shange, in *Boogie*, goes beyond the layers of physical and emotional paraphernelia of *For Colored Girls* into the subconscious black womanhood.

Each of her five published theatre pieces reveals Shange's careful blending of autobiographical threads with a comprehensive familiarity with her individual and collective racial and cultural ancestry. Arguing that timely pieces are important because the history of oppressed people is also oppressed like the people,[34] Shange, as a black feminist, embraces simultaneously and without personal choice, the intensively private and the aggressively public. For Shange, she and all writers of color have a responsiblity "to explore and document our lives. . . . Exploration leads to discovery and documentation leads to history. We need to have a very solid base of understanding about what we've come from and who we are."[35] It is against this wealthy background of historical information, political and creative possibilities that Shange establishes a place for an historically displaced community physically, artistically and psychologically.

Shange insists that Black women have no right to remain in this movement toward social and political change:

> A lot of black women don't want to accept our part of the responsibility for our oppression, and I'm just not free to do that. I will not look at my daughter 20 years from now and have her ask me "Well, why didn't you do something to help?" I feel obliged to pay attention to and to be an advocate for, in some artistic way that's satisfactory, the dramatic changes in attitude in the lives of women and children in this country.[36]

Childress, Hansberry, and Shange cannot be accused of writing only about domestic, narrow issues. Their scope is at once local, national and global. Their writings reveal a preoccupation with Africa, which shapes the content, conflicts, and tone of the bulk of their works. The family is the vehicle that allows these three women to express their feelings about the joys and sorrows facing the progeny of Africa. All three playwrights have written about families that, regardless of the many problems or obstacles, have survived and sometimes succeeded. One of the most important reasons why black families have been able to withstand slavery, reconstruction, urbanization, unemployment, and poverty is because of their adaptability of family roles. Where blood-related members of the black family create voids, the interactional or fictive members of the family provide the spirit, the history, and the courage that blacks need to sustain themselves in American society. There is a strong kinship that exists among blacks, one that links the blood-related family to other African-Americans and to their African ancestors. Jim Haskins, in "Some African Influences on the Afro-American Theater," contends: "As acquaintance with things Africa grows, as the essential and difficult work of tracing Africanism in America continues, we will come to know how really vast and invisible the African influence on all American theater has been."[37]

The black women playwrights of this study have drawn, both consciously and intuitively, upon African traditions to solidify their sense of the African-American family. Childress, Hansberry and Shange speak of the drums that beckon and prompt them to write of the heartbeat and the rhythms of a people whose single most important forte is its sense of family. Their quest for identity reveals a preoccupation with blacks turning to Africa for identity and viewing blacks around the world as a family.

NOTES

1. Pespsi Charles, transcriber, "Ntozake Shange Talks With Marcia Ann Gillespie," *Essence*, May 1985, 122-23.
2. Ntozake Shange, *Three Pieces* (New York: St. Martin's Press, 1981) ix.
3. Barbara Smith, "Towards a Black Feminist Criticism," *Conditions: Two* 1 (October 1977) 32.
4. Annette Kolodny, "Critical Response: The Feminist as Literary *Critic,*" *Critical Inquiry,* 2 (Summer 1976), 824-825. See also Cheris Kramer, Barrie Thorne, and Nancy Henley, "Perspectives on Language and Communication," *Signs,* 3 (Summer 1978) and Nelly Furman, "The Study of Women and Language: Comment on Vol. 3, no. 3," *Signs*, 4 (Autumn 1978).
5. Frantz Fanon, *A Dying Colonialism* (New York: Grove Press, 1967). Quoted in Ntozake Shange, *Three Pieces*, xii.
6. Sandra L. Richards "Conflicting Impulses in the Plays of Shange," *Black American Literature Forum*, vol. 17 (Summar 1983) 73
7. Seymour Reiter, *World Theater: The Structure and Meaning of Drama* (New York: Dek, 1973) 57-74
8. Kimberly W. Benston, "The Aesthetics of Modern Black Drama: From Mimesis to Methexis," in *The Theatre of Black Americans*, Vol. 1, ed.

Errol Hill (Englewood Cliffs, N.J.: Prentice Hall, 1980) 62-63.
9. Alvin Goldfarb and Edwin Wilson, *Living Theater: An Introduction to Theatre History* (New York: McGrawHill, 1983) 413
10. Ntozake Shange, *Three Pieces*. Excerpts from reviews of Shange's plays are found on the dust cover of this publication.
11. Kathleen Betsko and Rachel Koenig, "Ntozake Shange," *Interviews with Contemporary Women Playwrights* (New York: Beech Tree Books: a Quill Edition, 1987) 365
12. Barbara Christian, "The Contrary Women of Alice Walker: A Study of *In Love and Trouble," The Black Scholar,* 12 (Mar.-Apr. 1981) 21-30.
13. Sandra L. Richards, 76.
14. Ntozake Shange, *Three Pieces*, dust cover.
15. Details about the Koine Six stages of growth are based upon personal interviews with Lucius M. Guillory, educational consultant and principal of St. Gabriel's Catholic school in New Orleans La., and Revised Victor Cohea. M. Div. Pastor of St. Monica's Catholic Church, New Orleans La., July 1985. Cited in Elizabeth Brown-Guillory, *Their Place on the Stage: Black Women Playwrights in America* (New York: Greenwood Press, 1988) 81.
16. Edith Oliver, "The Theatre/Off-Broadway A Photograph and where the Missisippi Meets the Amazon," *New Yorker*, 2 Jan. 1978, 48.
17. Jean-Firancois Lyotard, "Answering the Question: What is Postmodernism?" trans. Regis Durand in *Innovation/Renovation: New Perspectives on the Humanities,* ed. Ihab and Sally Hassan (Madison: University of Wisconsin Press, 1983) 333
18. *Loc. cit.*
19. Sandra L. Richards, 75.
20. Margaret B. Wilkerson, ed., *9 Plays by Black Women* (New York: New American Library, 1986) 241.
21. C.W.E. Bigsby, *Beyond Broadway, Vol. 3 of A Critical Introduction to Twentieth Century American Drama* (New York: Cambridge University Press, 1985) 412.
22. Geneva Smitherman, in *Talkin and Testifyin: The Language of Black America* (Boston: Houghton Mifflin, 1977), reminds us that boogie woogie was also a popular dance style during the thirties. 256
23. Ntozake Shange, *Three Pieces*, dust cover.
24. Edward Mapp, "Black Women in Films, *The Black Scholar*, Vol. 13 (Summer 1982) 37.
25. *Ibid.*, 36.
26. Alice Childress. "The Negro Woman in American Literature," *Freedomways,* Vol. 6 (First Quarter 1966) 19.
27. Alice Childress, "The Negro Woman in American Literature," 19.
28. Mary Helen Washington, *Black-Eyed Susans: Classic Stories by and about Black Women* (New York: The Anchor Books, 1975) xx-xxi.
29. Barbara Molette, "Black Women Playwrights: They Speak Who Listens?" *Black World,* Vol. 25 (April 1976) 28-34.

30. Claudia Tate, *Black Women Writers at Work* (New York: Continuum, 1982) 157.
31. Andrew Billingsley, *Black Families in White America* (Englewood Cliffs, N.J: Prentice Hall, 1968) 24.
32. Judith Weinraub, "A Touring Black Troupe Begins Its Journey," *Washington Star,* 15 June 1980, HI.
33. Ntozake Shange, Foreword to *Three Pieces,* xi.
34. Ntozake Shange, Arts and Education Council's Conference on Southern Literature, University of Tennessee at Chattanooga (4 April 1987).
35. H. Maria Noel, "Ntozake Shange writes Characters, Not Messages," *Chattanooga Times,* 4 April 1987, B2.
36. Jewelle Gomez, *Belles Lettres*, Interview: Ntozake Shange, *Belles Letters: A Review of Books by Women,* September/October 1985, 9.
37. James Haskins, "Some African Influences on the Afro-American Theatre," in *The Theatre of Black Americans*, ed. Errol Hill, 28-29.

Conclusion

Alice Childress, Lorraine Hansberry, and Ntozake Shange are three outstanding black women playwrights who are crucial links in the development of black women playwriting in America. These three playwrights offer perspectives and portraits of black life and culture which are decidedly different from those of black male and white playwrights. They dispel the myths of the "contented slave," "the tragic mulatto," "the comic Negro," "the exotic primitive," and the faithful servant singing the spiritual. They have created images of the blacks such as "the black militant," "the black assimilationist," "the struggling black artist" and "the contemporary black matriarch." As Elizabeth Brown Guillory points out, the images which distinctively appear in the plays of these playwrights are "the black male in search of his manhood" and "the black male as a walking wounded."[1]

Genevieve Fabre points out that Alice Childress's plays can be placed in the category of ethnic theatre of black experience as opposed to militant theatre of protest.[2] The theatre of experience develops out of a dialogue in the language of black about their own experience. This theatre, which is both collective and individual, embraces the rituals of daily life. It derives its strength from the liturgy of the black church, religious and secular music, and the oral tradition. It offers a contrast to the didactic speech of the militant theatre which demonstrates and prescribes action. It does not advocate change in the condition of the blacks. This theatre illustrates the existence of a black culture that continually invents itself outside the codes of the dominant society. It perceives black culture as a body of knowledge and as a symbolic universe. Interacting with a language which is distinctively black, these images of black culture articulate ethnic identity. Facets of black culture revealed here through the dynamics of theatricalization cannot be considered as those of a sub-culture or a counter-culture. Envisaging black culture as a sub-culture or a counter-culture would involve defining it too simplistically as a reaction to a dominant culture.

One of the important features of African-American playwriting is that in their quest for identity dramatized by these playwrights the problem of ties with Africa occupies an important place at two levels: at the level of thematic preoccupations and at the level of design of the drama including choreography, miming, dance and ritual and other features which are derived from the African world view. Two images converge here. They are (1) of a mythic land belonging to a distant past and revived by collective memory (2) of a real continent of nations struggling for liberation. The African-American theatre, by means of its plea for liberation and by means of its incorporation of features from the oral traditions of Africa, is a forum for the expression of social roles around which images of the new identity are carved. The theatre is seen as both the manifestation and the formulation of culture. In performance, it transforms the audience into privileged actors seized by the glare of history.

In his essay, "Black Theatre—Go Home," Ron Milner appeals to his fellow playwrights to create a living art from material and techniques within the community. He defines theatre as a prism of life that projects warnings, directions, memories, or exemplary creations. From his point of view, the theatre not merely reflects experience but gives organization and meaning to the confusion of reality. Ed Bullins visualizes the theatre as a monument built from black awareness. Defined in nationalistic and religious terms, the theatre is transformed into a place of communion and of celebration dedicated to the creation of communal forms.[3]

For the playwright and theoretician Paul Carter Harrison, theatre expresses the spiritual reality of African-American life. The theatre of experience, by finding its roots further back in African oral traditions, reveals two features: (1) The dynamism of a culture whose importance and authenticity have been denied, and (2) Integration of all aspects of black life. The mode of discourse develops from dramatizations found in black tradition—religion, rituals, narrative forms and music. It borrows most of its elements from popular culture but enlarges that culture by proposing specific models, images and new representations of reality.

The militant theatre and the theatre of experience are not two successive stages in the development of black drama. The theatre of experience was born out of the disenchantment caused by the defeat of the revolutionary fervour. In examining the struggle of the blacks, militant theatre focuses on the condition of the victims and also shows the possibilities for change. It revives in its dramaturgy the earlier traditions of slave narratives, popular epics, and abolitionist literature. The theatre of experience finds its roots further back in African oral traditions. The two developments reveal two distinct perspectives. The militant theatre subordinates theatre to an action by making it serve the revolutionary cause; the theatre of experience restores the theatre's primordial function and autonomy. It offers a more comprehensive definition of black theatre. Sometimes its ideological choice of a focus on black people by black playwrights for black audiences makes it merge with the revolutionary theatre.

The Moynihan report describes the persistent failure of blacks to create stable family units. If the society depends on the institution of the family, then the deterioration of the black family leads to the death of the community. The Moynihan report is an example of white liberals' attempt to legislate on black community. While being ignorant of its social fabric and culture, black theatre could not remain apart from this debate. It raised issues central to the whole question of the black family. The black family is looked upon as a dynamic cultural entity endowed with its own vitality. The dialectical relations it maintains with other elements of the community and with the dominant society are the subject of dramatization.

Lorraine Hansberry's *A Raisin in the Sun* provides the most interesting prototype of the black family ever developed in the contemporary theatre. Hansberry endows the Younger family with characteristics that challenge the existing stereotypes. The Youngers seem to be exceptional and separate from the mass of family types in the ghetto. Like those of many African-Americans, the Youngers' forbears left for the North in search of employment and a life free from racism. Hansberry makes the relations between the characters really dramatic by introducing a moment of crisis when each dreams of spending the dead father's insurance annuity in his or her own way. These different aspirations reveal divergent ethical choices. *Raïsin* illustrates social and racial relations in America which promise integration in theory only. On a more profound level, however, the Youngers' victory is due to the fact that they are different from others in the ghetto. They have adopted the values of the middle class and hence they deserve to move into the white suburbs. The Youngers' aspiration to get out of the ghetto characterizes the aspiration of many ghetto families. But the Youngers' entry into the white neighbourhood and Hansberry's hope for integration for the Youngers and for Black theatre can only be a concession to the taste and ideology of Broadway audiences.

This theme of integration is presented more realistically in Louis Peterson's *Take a Giant Step*, a play which depicts the life of a black family after the move. Neither Hansberry nor Peterson states that integration could be a trap for blacks for, in effect, social mobility leads them into a hostile environment and exiles them from their community. However, *A Raisin in the Sun* marks an important step in the direction of the image of the family which black drama presents. The play's interest lies especially in the representation of relations between man and woman and in the contradictory images Hansberry proposes. Walter gives us a portrait of the mother wherein he offers criticism of the down-to-earth woman:

> Man say to his woman: I got me a dream. His woman say: Eat your eggs. Man say I got to take hold of this here world baby. And a woman will say: Eat your eggs and go to work. Man say: I got to change my life, I'm choking to death, baby! And his woman say—your eggs is getting cold. . . . That is just what is wrong with the colored woman in this world. . . . Don't understand about building their men up and making 'em feel like they somebody. Like they can do something.[6]

In the theatre of the sixties, this role is more clearly defined as that of a castrator, and the woman will appear quite often as an obstacle to the man's affirmation of virility. *A Raisin in the Sun*, by an analysis of moral considerations rather than the economic situation, presents a conclusion where perseverance and integrity triumph. And Broadway audiences preferred to call this play not a black play but an American play.

The realist playwright, according to Lorraine Hansberry, states not only what is but what can and should be. Accepting realism as a mode of dramatic unfolding, she expresses in her plays both her American identity and the black female identity of one who grew up in a comfortable home on the Southside of Chicago. There is perhaps no exaggeration in the statement, when we examine the entire canon of Lorraine Hansberry's writings, that she is the voice not merely of black identity but of the dynamic culture and the tortured politics of the United States of America as a whole. This is revealed in a play like *The Sign in Sidney Brustein's Window* with its challenging of the apathy of the American intellectual and his indifference to the serious problems overtaking the world. In fact, Hansberry shows how the obligation to limit one's creative energies to the treatment of the immediate but parochial injustices of racial intolerance has indeed sapped the creative vitality of the black writer. In thus achieving an objectivity and a perspective which free her from entanglement in a one-sided particularity, Lorraine Hansberry is no more separate and apart from America than one can think of Cyprian Ekwensi apart from the Nigeria which is embodied, symbolized and illuminated in his writing. In this, Hansberry is not an exotic ethnic of the

Eurocentric imagination. Her vision is essentially harmonizing and intergrating.

Hansberry's substantial contribution seems to be to reveal a shared vision with Alice Childress and Ntozake Shange. An examination of the symbols of these playwrights indicates a conscious effort on their part to illuminate the condition of the blacks in patriarchal America through the medium of a "Theatre of Struggle" in which black resiliency and spirit of survival are heralded. While Alice Childress confronts social and political issues out of a philosophical conviction that all art is and must be political, Hansberry believes that the black artist has a responsibility to tell the truth, especially about the coloured. But in terms of mediating this vision through the theatrical medium, she is committed to the idea of celebrating the joy of living and struggling together and optimistically reconstructing the world. A study of the symbolism of *A Raisin in the Sun* and *The Drinking Gourd* would illustrate this idea. *A Raisin in the Sun*, for example, suggests through the symbol of the furnishings on the stage a spirit of desperation associated with the ghetto image. In her *To Be Young Gifted and Black* Hansberry writes: "We must come out of the ghettos of America, because the ghettos are killing us; not only our dreams but our very bodies."[7] The furnishings suggest two things: the struggle of the blacks and the deferred dreams. In addition, the image of the ghetto and the feeble plant contribute, in terms of theatrical suggestiveness, the idea of deprivation, thwarted dreams and so on. These manipulations of the "tonal form" indicate how, like Shange who shapes tonal form in the choreopoem, *For Colored Girls*, Lorraine Hansberry not only portrays the spirit of survival of the blacks but also their movement towards something liberating and dynamic.

A Raisin in the Sun, although dismissed as assimilationist, projects a revealing portrait of the African-American family and its struggle for equality. In the words of Anne Cheney, *Raisin* not only stresses the importance of African roots, but also progresses into a "universal representation of all people's hopes, fears and dreams." In examining the importance of African roots, Hansberry not only anticipates the new thinking of the 60s but also resurrects the idea of the Harlem Renaissance. The very title of the play, derived from Langston Hughes, suggests the tensions and frustrations of the black man's and the black woman's existence by an evocation of the images of inevitable decay and deferred dreams. If Walter Lee represents the ambitions, frustrations, and at the same time, the dream of attaining equality with the whites by imitating their mode of social advancement, and thus ironically promotes the white racist cause, Beneatha's personal odyssey towards wholeness culminating in the African dance introduces yet another tonal quality in the play whereby an establishment of kinship with African roots is suggested. Beneatha's intense awareness of her racial origins and her association with Asagai indicate, through her wearing of the African robes, how she steeps herself in the culture of her forbears. The nickname "Alaiyo" given to Beneatha is an indication that Hansberry's concern in this play is not so much with the poverty of the Youngers but with the need for spiritual replenishment and the return of dignity to the blacks. In a way, Asagai illustrates a concept (which gained momentum during Marcus Garvey's "Back to Africa" movement) by inculcating in Beneatha a growing awareness of the need to fight for black people's rights and for women's rights. He thus demonstrates to her the idea of black is beautiful. In fact, Asagai himself is not only a symbol of black struggle and freedom, but even more, a symbol of the oneness of suffering either in Africa or black America. Asagai's serving as a cultural conduit whereby he baptizes Beneatha in African history and mores shows yet another element of the African-American drama, employed in *A Raisin in the Sun* to some extent but utilized more fully as a dramatic device in *The Drinking Gourd* which belongs to the ritual tradition of African-American drama. One of the qualities of this tradition is that within the context of real and present time and place, the audience participate in the dramatic event by means of their emphatic transportation to their roots. As against this dramatic device, the Euro-American tradition aims at creating, in a mimetic sense, an illusion of reality of time, place, and character where there is an architectural separation of actors from audience. The elements of the black ritual drama that are subtly interfused with the dramatic design of Hansberry's last plays celebrate a sense of community and fellowship which is one of the characteristics of a drama embodying a quest for identity. If *Les Blancs* examines the implications of the Mau Mau Revolution, *The Drinking Gourd* is an incisive indictment of American slavery which has proved itself to be an exploitative self-perpetuating system.

As in Soyinka's plays, in which the Yoruba myths offer a mytho-dramatic design, in *Les Blancs* the popular mythic symbolism of the hyenas and the elephants is used in order to highlight the idea of intrusion. The cause of total African self-rule and freedom is suggested by the theme of the Mau Mau Revolution which is treated in Ngugi's novels like *Weep Not Child* and plays like *The Trial of Dedan Kimathi.* Not only does Lorraine Hansberry use African myths to suggest the idea of rites of passage, but she also employs old folk tales in order to heighten the drama of revolution and change. In *Les Blancs,* Kumalo, the returned expatriate, and Tshembe, who finally recognizes the value of revolution, are in a way the two Kenyattas.

The Drinking Gourd shows the relentless greed and exploitation and unresponsiveness operating in the abuse of the system of slavery. The play is a costume drama which projects yet another aspect of not only the blackness but the universality of Hansberry. While the play takes its title from a Negro spiritual, it gives expression to Hansberry's view of the Slave South as dehumanizing both the black and the white with its characteristic capitalistic infrastructure. Through the portrayal of Hiram in this play, Hansberry seems to indicate that the insidious effects of slavery will be far reaching. At the end of the play, the Soldier/Narrator says: "Slavery is beginning to cost this nation a lot. It has become a drag on the great industrial nation we are determined to become; it lags a full century behind the great American notion of one strong federal union which our eighteenth-century founders knew was the only way we could eventually become one of the powerful nations of the world. . . . It is possible that slavery might destroy itself—but it is more possible that it would destroy these United States first."[10]

The portrayal of Rissa in *The Drinking Gourd* shows how Hansberry breaks the mold shaped by southern attitudes and manages to bring a new life to the cliche depiction of the black mother. Rissa flagrantly turns her back on Hiram in desperation and continues to minister to her blind son. This shows that Hansberry reverses the sacred image of the mother in this play and inspires her nevertheless with a motherly act of vengeance which sets her apart from the familiar archetype.

A play of ideas, *The Sign in Sidney Brustein's Window* is a new theatrical experiment interweaving nevertheless the familiar constituent elements of Lorraine Hansberry's drama. The play challenges the apathy of the American intellectual. Set in a time of racial turmoil, it reflects a spirit of harmony and acceptance between blacks and whites and among peoples of varied background. The play is more or less in the main stream of contemporary drama. Relating itself to the American tradition at large and further locating itself within the tradition of Absurd drama, this play however reveals a typical attribute of Hansberry's work in general in its mixing of individual and social drama, European and African culture, realism and fantasy, drama and dance and music, and tragedy and comedy. There is the fantasy sequence in the play in which Sidney's wife Iris dances to banjo music

Completed in 1962, Hansberry's most experimental piece *What Use Are Flowers?* is a fantasy about nuclear holocaust and the possibilities of survival. The play deals with the theme of civilizing children orphaned by nuclear holocaust. The play's stress on the educational theme links it up with the African tradition and shows that education is a redeeming, rejuvenating force contributing vitally not only to the expression of freedom but also to the restoration of humanity.

In late 1962, Lorraine Hansberry proposed a community theatre project for Harlem. In this prospectus for the John Brown Memorial Theatre of Harlem, she came out with the suggestion that this theatre should carve out the cultural heritage of the people by showing its inextricable links with African ancestry. At the same time, however, she suggested that this theatre should "readily, freely and with the spirit of creativity of all mankind, also utilize all and any forces of the western heritage of that same people in the arts." Hansberry's plays indeed reveal this assimilation in an abundant measure. In fact, the very act of naming a black community theatre after a white man emphasizes the consciously paradoxical nature of Hansberry's world view and art: she is a fighter for her race who insists on the oneness of the cause of humanity, a Pan-Africanist who wishes to place the western heritage of African-Americans alongside the African heritage, and a dramatist who is both an artist and a propagandist.

Alice Childress's plays, which Genevieve Fabre places in the category of "ethnic theatre of black experience" as opposed to the militant theatre of protest, are a crucial link in the development of black women's playwriting. She incorporates in her plays the liturgy of the black church, traditional music, African mythology, folklore and fantasy, apart from experimenting with socio-political, romantic, biographical, historical, and feminist themes. A forerunner of Lorraine Hansberry, Sonia Sanchez, Martie Charles, Adrienne Kennedy, Ntozake Shange and others, Childress has opened the door for other black women playwrights to make significant dramaturgical advances. It has been pointed out by Elizabeth Brown Guillory that Childress, by her refusal to bow down before the pressures of commercialism and by her insistence on craft and integrity, has paved the way for significant and innovative contributions to black women playwriting in America. She provides the bread and song of the plays especially of Lorraine Hansberry and Ntozake Shange. Childress's sensitive treatment of the black male in search of his manhood reflects her vision that black men and women can become whole only when they join forces and resources as well. Unlike the black male in search of his manhood is the black male "as a walking wounded."[13] Here in this instance the black male struggles to free himself and others from oppressive forces. He possesses a positive sense of self and a strong sense of family togetherness which his African forbears brought with them to America. In short, this character is the opposite of the image of the incorrigible black beast that dominated the American stage for decades. The best example of the black male as a walking wounded is Hannibal in Hansberry's *The Drinking Gourd*. Hannibal refuses to accept slavery and makes a vehement pronouncement:

> And I tell you like I tell Coffin (the plantation Uncle Tom)—I am the only kind of slave I could be—a bad one! Every day that come and hour that pass that I got sense to make a half step do for a whole; every day that I can pretend sickness 'stead of health; to be stupid, 'stead of smart, lazy 'stead of quick—I aims to do it. And the more pain it give your Marster and the more it cost him—the more Hannibal be a man![14]

Hannibal embodies the survival spirit of blacks in America and shows Hansberry's perspective as societal and global. Hansberry once said that she was concerned that her plays treat issues that were highly sociopolitical:

> All art is ultimately social: that which agitates and that which prepares the mind for slumber . . . The writer is deceived who thinks he has some other choice. The question is not whether one will make a social statement in one's work—but only what the statement will say, for if it says anything, it will be social.[15]

Though Childress, Hansberry and Shange have created credible images of black men, the females in their plays are more subtly delineated. These writers do not limit themselves to the deity or slut syndrome. They offer a special view of black women. It is from this point of view that there is a special justification for studying black women writers:

> What is most important about the black woman writer is her special and unique vision of the black woman. . . . One of the main preoccupations of the black woman writer has been the black woman herself—her aspirations, her conflicts, her relationships to her men and her children, her creativity. . . . That these writers have first-hand knowledge of their subject ought to be enough to command attention.[16]

One image which dominates the plays of Childress, Hansberry, and Shange is the evolving black woman. Rissa in *The Drinking Gourd* by moving from mammy to militancy epitomizes the evolving black woman. In Shange's *For Colored Girls* the women are preoccupied with themselves because they have been disappointed by the men who have come into their lives. The image of the black woman in Childress's *Wine in the Wilderness* and Shange's *For Colored Girls* is that of one who has to "sing the blues" before she is able to make some sense of the chaos in her life. Though the abandoned black in Childress and Shange bewail their loss emphasis is placed on their ability to survive in a world where they are forced to care for themselves. Shange's feminist play *For Colored Girls* is different from either a Childress play or a Hansberry play. It advocates that women band together to shield themselves from the enemy men. The evolving black women in Shange's *For Colored Girls* speak of the brutal treatment accorded to them by men. These women have been knocked down, but they search for a way to hold on to their sanity and to improve their lifestyles. They show the spirit of survival, realize their responsibility to themselves, as lady in blue demonstrates. As Elizabeth Brown-Guillory observes, "Shange's women are not whole; they are bruised women in transition who are apparently forming another sub-culture."[17] Alice Childress, Lorraine Hansberry and Ntozake Shange are black women playwrights who do not create images which represent the majority of blacks. They do however present a vital slice of life and capture a multitude of images of the blacks.

In order to develop the artistic and ideological basis for a new drama, black theatre establishes strong ties with African-American culture. Combining the three principles of drum, song and dance, the theatre associates textual with scenic writing. From the Harlem Renaissance to the sixties, theoreticians of black art have always envisaged a relation between theatre and culture. The theatre has been viewed as a means to rediscover, recapture, and reinvent the cultural heritage. It is a space where people can be confronted by their history and antiquity. In dramatic discourse, the past becomes a syntagmatic element of the total history of African-Americans. The theatre shows blacks as a people and a nation. Since a recapturing of cultural consciousness is at the core of black ideology, models for forging a new theatrical language are sought within that very culture. Certain elements borrowed from the oral, musical, or religious traditions or from rituals of daily life are integrated into the drama as a morphology, a structure or a sign system. These elements codify the aesthetics of the theatre and create a new art form which goes beyond the dictates of Western dramaturgy. Apart from incorporating the oral tradition which holds a prominent place in African-American culture and which transmits a sense of the collective consciousness, music and ritual are employed in order to suggest a sense of community and in order to create an "atmosphere" in the theatre suffused in black heritage and identity. Just as religious dance came to serve a secular function, secular dance too preserves its ritualistic character. The incorporation of dance into drama, the theatricality, the visual effect and the symbolic force it represents shows how in African-American drama the element of dance blurs the distinction between spectators and participants. One of the important elements in the plays of Shange is its choreography. In drama, choreography can revive the principal moments in the history of the black nation: confrontation, encounter, dispersal and resistance. The element of dance inspires the work of many theatrical groups. The most noteworthy direction has been taken by Gilbert Moses in *Slave Ship* and in the dramatizations of Ntozake Shange. The revolution in the black theatre in the sixties and the seventies has shown how the theatre postulates the existence of a community of experiences and becomes a space where they can be represented.

The theatre in the hands of Ntozake Shange views temporality as a double dimension. It refers to the individual's moment of psychological commitment and to the group's historical and mythical past.

In *For Colored Girls*, Shange expresses her commitment to women and children who are abused every year. Unequivocally this work presents men as the instruments of pain. One important symbol in *For Colored Girls* that legitimizes women's vision is the array of colours worn by the seven women. The rainbow myth illustrates that these coloured women are moving towards something good, liberating, and dynamic. Dancing is another symbol that shapes the tonal form of the choreopoem. It launches Shange's characters on self-discovery, initiation into womanhood. Shange writes, "With dance I discovered my body more intimately than I had imagined possible . . . pulling ancient trampled spirits out of present tense Afro-American dance."[18]

With *For Colored Girls* Shange brought to the American stage a distinctively black feminist perspective. The perspective is manifested in the form of the choreopoem which is interdisciplinary in nature and non-Eurocentric in its texture and expression of African-American culture.

The Choreopoem for Shange is not necessarily meant to challenge the existing Europeon forms of art. It is a form which allows her characters to celebrate themselves. It is further a form through which she is able to declare war on partriarchy's universally oppressive system. The choreopoem for Shange is a mode of empowerment at women whereby they not only recall, but aggressively participate in a cultural war of aesthetics as it were.

Shange carved out for herself a place in American theatre history when she successfully "broadened and redefined American theatre to include the choreopoem as an acceptable, legitimate dramatic form. Not only did she popularize the choreopoem, but she brought to the American theater an art that is undeniably African. Shange's choreopoem, like

African theatre is comprised of chants, poetry, dance and rituals."[19]

Shange's use of the "Choreopoem" form is complex and innovative. C.W.E. Bigsby offers an historical context of her Choreopoem: "The essence of black poetry, particularly in the 1960s and early 1970s, had lain in its public nature, its performatics. It was never a closet poetry (unless, as LeRoi Jones once observed, the closet be "as wide as God's eye"). Sonia Sanchez, Nikki Giovanni and many others performed their poetry at large public gatherings in which the symbiosis between audience and performer was a vital part of the aesthetic. Such occasions shared something of the atmosphere of the store-front church. They trembled, in other words, on the brink of ritual and of theatre. Shange's choreopoem is a natural extension of this. Poems with music and dance, forming a narrative account, become a play."[21]

Bigsby acknowledges Shange's contribution to the theatre when he says that in *For Colored Girls* Shange presents "a collage of experiences ranging from love to abortion to rape and from ecstasy to despair."[20] Feminist poemplays, Shange's pieces inform women that they have a responsibility to love themselves and each other enough to resist oppression. Her female characters battle with the incomprehensible dilemma of living in a world where being female and coloured makes them twice oppressed. Convinced that American patriarchy often denies injustices committed against women, Shange sketches the lives of often mutilated heroines who band together to provide each other with the courage to become self-sufficient and self-loving to survive. Thus Shange portrays the black spirit of survival and quest for identity in her plays. Shange's trilogy, *Three Pieces*, explores the notion that a person's identity is not defined by things but by a belief in self. *A Photograph: Lovers in Motion* presents this theme through the central character, Sean David, a struggling novice photographer involved with a complex triad of women. *Spell # 7* celebrates the joy, pride and horror of blackness. Shange's most experimental dramatic piece *Boogie Woogie Landscape*s offers a fine blend of surrealism and expressionism to create a fantasy world in which Layla and the other night life companions sing, dance, and share emotional moments of being black and female in America. Employing feminist rhetoric and evocative poetry and blending music, dance, and poetry to express the misery and ecstasy of being female and black in America, Shange is one of the finest of African-American playwrights who have forged a new dramatic idiom to capture the nuances of being black in America. With her keen ear for black American idioms recreated in the rhythms and nuances of the language of her characters, Shange recalls some of the salient features of the American theatre and establishes a vital link between African theatre and the African-American experience. Her interest is in the poetry of the moment and the emotional and aesthetic impact of a character. In her search for the African-American theatre that suits her dramatic concerns and her quest for identity, Shange offers a recreation in the theatre of an African-American language which expresses the self-conscious feelings of the community creating an African-American image in its essential truth. In her quest for the African theatre that suits her genius, she uses the theatre, as Alvin Goldfarb and Edwin Wilson point out, not in the European theatrical manner of entertaining and teaching but in the African model of "embodying, affecting, and being."[22] Shange insists that her background shaped her view of the interconnectedness of African-Americans and other people of colour: "My parents have always been especially involved in all kinds of Third World culture. . . . I was always aware that there were different kinds of black people all over the world because my father had friends from virtually all of the colonized French-, Spanish- and English-speaking countries. So I knew I wasn't on this planet by myself. I had some connection with other people."[23] Informed by an African world view, Shange reveals a preoccupation with blacks as an integral part of the African continuum.

Shange, like Kennedy, is less concerned with resolving conflicts particularly between European and African influences on African-American female identity. Shange's characters find hope, not deterioration and despair, in their racially segregated worlds.

Lorraine Hansberry and Ntozake Shange, along with Alice Childress, have carved out a unique place for themselves on the American stage by being vital links in the evolution of black theatre in America. If Hansberry's 1959 Broadway debut of *A Raisin in the Sun* made black theatre fashionable and marketable, Shange's explosive choreopoem of 1976 broadened black theatre to include a quest for sexual, racial and social identity. The dramaturgical advances made by the three playwrights Childress, Hansberry and Shange are "as interdependent as African-Americans are to their African counterparts."[24] This is a subject prominent in the works of all the three women writers. And especially in Hansberry and Shange's dramaturgy it adds an intra-mural quality.

NOTES

1. Elizabeth Brown Guillory, "Black Women Playwrights: Exorcising Myths," Phylon Quarterly, Vol. XLVIII, No. 3, 1987) 229.

2. Genevieve Fabre, *Drumbeats, Masks and Metaphor: Contemporary Afro-American Theatre* (Cambridge, Mass.: Harvard University Press, 1983) 3.
3. Ed. Bullins, "Preface" to *The Theme is Blackness* (New York: Morrow, 1973) 12 ff.
4. Paul Carter Harrison, *The Drama of Nommo* (New York: Grove Press, 1972).
5. The Negro Family: The Case for National Action (Washington, D.C.: V.S. Govt. Printing Office, March 1965). Cited in Genevieve Fabre, 125.
6. Lorraine Hansberry, *A Raisin in the Sun* (New York: Random House, 1959) 15.
7. Lorraine Hansberry, *To Be Young Gifted and Black.* Adapted by Robert Nemiroff (New York: New American Library, 1969) 131-32.
8. Stanley Vincent Longman, *Composing Drama for Stage and Screen* (Boston , Mass.: Allyn and Bacon, 1986) 119.
9. Anne Cheney, *Lorraine Hansberry* "Measure Him Right: *A Raisin in the Sun*" (Virginia Polytechnic Institute and State University, 1984) 55.
10. Robert Nemiroff, ed., *Lorraine Hansberry: The Collected Last Plays* (New York: New American Library, 1972) 217.
11. Steven R. Carter, "The John Brown Theatre: Lorraine Hansberry's Cultural Views and Dramatic Goals," *Freedomways,* Fourth Quarter, 1979, 186.
12. Genevieve Fabre, 3.
13. Elizabeth Brown Guillory, 229.
14. Lorraine Hansberry, *The Drinking Gourd*, in *Black Theater, U.S.A.: Forty-Five Plays by Black Americans, 1847-1974*, ed. James V. Hatch and Ted Shine (New York, 1974) 728.
15. Margaret B. Wilkerson, "The Sighted Eyes and Feeling Heart of Lorraine Hansberry," *Black American Literature Forum,* 17 (Spring 1983) 9.
16. Mary Helen Washington, *Black-Eyed Susans: Classic Stories by and about Black Women* (New York, 1975) X.
17. Elizabeth Brown Guillory, 238.
18. Ntozake Shange, *For Colored Girls Who Have Considered Suicide/When the Rainbow is Enuf* (New York: Bantam Books, 1977) xv-xvi.
19. Elizabeth Brown Guillory, *Their Place on the Stage Black Women Playwrights in America,* Contributions in Afro-American and African Studies, No. 117 (New York: Greenwood Press, 1988) 41.
20. C.W.E. Bigsby, *Beyond Broadway,* Vol. 3, *A Critical Introduction to Twentieth Century American Drama* (New York: Cambridge University Press, 1985) 411-12.
21. *Ibid.*, 411.
22. Alvin Goldfarb and Edwin Wilson, *Living Theater: An Introduction to Theater History* (New York: McGraw Hill, 1983) 413.
23. Claudia Tate, *Black Women Writers at Work* (New York: (Continuum, 1982) 157.
24. Elizabeth Brown Guillory, *Their Place on the Stage*, 46.

Bibliography

Primary Sources

Hansberry, Lorraine. *A Raisin in the Sun*. New York: Random House, 1959.

The Sign in Sidney Brustein's Window: A Drama in Three Acts. New York: Random House, 1965.

The Collected Last Plays (*Les Blancs, The Drinking Gourd, What Use Are Flowers?*). Edited with Critical Background by Robert Nemiroff. Introduction by Margaret B. Wilkerson. Foreword and Afterword by Julius Lester. New York: New American Library, 1983.

A Raisin in the Sun and *The Sign in Sidney Brustein's Window*. New York: New American Library, 1966.

"The Drinking Gourd." In *Black Theatre U.S.A.: Forty-Five Plays by Black Americans, 1847-1974*, ed. James V. Hatch and Ted Shine. New York: The Free Press, 1974, 728.

Les Blancs: The Collected Last Plays of Lorraine Hansberry, ed. Robert Nemiroff. New York: Vintage Books, 1973.

Childress, Alice. *Florence, A One Act Drama*. *Masses and Mainstream,* Vol. 3, October 1950. 34-47.

Childress, Alice. *Wine in the Wilderness*. In *Black Theatre U.S.A.* 738-55.

______. *Wine in the Wilderness*. New York: Dramatists Play Service, 1969.

______. *Mojo* and *String*. New York: Dramatists Play Service, 1971.

______. *Wedding Band*. New York: Samuel French, 1973.

Shange, Ntozake. *For Colored Girls Who Have Considered Suicide/ When the Rainbow is Enuf*. New York: Macmillan, Bantam Books, 1980.

______. *Three Pieces* (*Spell # 7, A Photograph: Lovers in Motion, Boogie Woogie Landscapes*). New York: St. Martin's Press, 1981.

______. *From Okra to Greens/ A Different Kinda Love Story: A Play with Music & Dance*. New York: Samuel French, 1985.

Secondary Sources

Armah, Ayi Kwei. *Two Thousand Seasons*. Chicago: Third World Press, 1979.

Bakhtin, Mikhail, ed. "Discourse in the Novel." Reprinted in Michael Holquist, ed., *The Dialogic Imagination: Four Essays by M.M. Bakhtin*. Austin: University of Texas Press, 1981.

Bambara, Toni Cade. "Commitment: Toni Cade Bambara Speaks." *Sturdy Black Bridges: Visions of Black Women in Literature,* ed. R. P. Bell *et al.* New York: Anchor Press, 1979.

Beckett, Samuel. *Endgame*. London: Faber, 1958.

______. *Waiting For Godot*. New York: Grove Press, 1978.

Benston, Kimberly W. "The Aesthetics of Modern Black Drama From Mimesis to Methexis." *The Theatre of Black Americans*, ed. Errol Hill. Englewood Cliffs, N.J.: Prentice Hall, 1980.

Betsko, Kathleen and Rachel Koenig. "Ntozake Shange." *Interviews with Contemporary Women Playwrights*. New York: Beech Tree Books: a Quill Edition, 1987.

Bigsby, C.W.E. *Beyond Broadway*. Vol. 3 of *A Critical lntroduction to Twentieth Century American Drama*. New York: Cambridge University Press, 1985.

Billilngsley, Andrew. *Black Families in White America*. Englewood Cliffs, N.J.: Prentice Hall, 1968.

Brown Guillory, Elizabeth. *Their Place on the Stage: Black Women Playwrights in America*. Contributions in Afro-American and African Studies, No. 117. New York: Greenwood Press, 1988.

Brown, Elizabeth. "Ntozake Shange." *Afro-American Writers after 1955: Dramatists and Prose Writers*, Vol. 38 of *Dictionary of Literary Biography*, Detroit, 1985.

Brown, Sterling. *Negro Poetry and Drama*. Washington D.C The Associates in Negro Folk Education, 1937.

Bullins, Ed. "Preface," *The Theme is Blackness*. New York: Morrow, 1973, 12 ff.

Carter, Steven R. *Hansberry's Drama: Commitment amid Complexity*. Urbana and Chicago: University of Illinois Press, 1991.

Cheney, Anne. *Lorraine Hansberry*. "Measure Him Right: *A Raisin in the Sun*." Virginia Polytechnic Institute and State University, 1984.

Childress, Alice. *Black Women Writers: 1950-1980*. Ed. Mari Evans. New York: Anchor Press/Doubleday, 1984.

Chinoy, Helen Rich and Linda Walsh Jenkiins. *Women in American Theatre*. New York: Crown Publishers, 1981.

Chinweizu, Onwucheckwa Jemie and Ihechukwe Madubuike. "African Fiction and Poetry and Their Critics," *Toward the Decolonization of African Literature*. Washington D.C.: Howard University Press, 1983.

Cruse, Harold. *The Crisis of the Negro Intellectual*. New York: William Morrow, 1967.

Danneth, Sylvia. *20th Century: Profiles of Negro Womanhood*, Yonkers, N.Y.:

Educational Heritage, 1966.

Davis, Arthur. P. and Michael W. Peplow, ed. *The New Negro Renaissance*. New York: Holt, Rinehart and Winston, 1975.

Dianne, Herman. "The Rape Culture. " Jo Freeman, ed., *Women: A Feminist Perspective*. Palo Alto: Mayfield, 1975.

Eliot, T.S. *The Use of Poetry and Use of Criticism*. London: Faber and Faber, 1933.

Esslin, Martin. *The Theatre of the Absurd*, 3rd ed. Harmondsworth: Penguin, 1987.

Fabre, Genevieve. *Afro-American Poetry and Drama. 1760-1975.* Detroit, Mich: Book Tower, 1979.

______. *Drumbeats, Masks and Metaphor: Contemporary Afro-American Theatre*, Boston, Mass.: Harvard University Press, 1983.

Fanon, Frantz. *A Dying Colonialism*. New York: Grove Press, 1967.

Gates, Louis, ed. *"Race" Writing and Difference*. Chicago University of Chicago Press, 1986.

Goldfarb, Alvin and Edwin Wilson. *Living Theater: An Introduction to Theater History*. New York: McGraw-Hill, 1983.

Hansberry, Lorraine. *To Be Young Gifted and Black*. Englewood Cliffs, New York: Prentice Hall, 1969.

Harrison, Paul Carter. *The Drama of Nommo*. New York: Grove Press, 1972.

Haskins, James. "Some African Influences on the Afro-American Theatre." *The Theater of Black Americans*, ed. Errol Hill. Englewood Cliffs, N.J.: Prentice Hall, 1980.

Hay, Samuel. *Black Women Writers: 1950-1980*, ed. Mari Evans. New York: Anchor Press/Doubleday, 1984.

Hughes, Langston. "Mother to Son," "Harlem" in *American Literature Survey: The Twentieth Century*. Ed. Milton R. Stern and Seymour L. Gross, 1962. Revised Edition. New Delhi: Light and Life Publishers, 1975.

Jones, LeRoi (Amiri Baraka). *About Blues, Blues People*. New York: William Morrow, 1963.

Jordon, June. *Civil Wars*, Boston: Beacon Press, 1981.

Livingston, James T. *Caribbean Rhythms : The Emerging English Literature of the West Indies*. Ed. James T. Livingston. New York: Pocket Books, 1974.

Longman, Stanley Vincent. *Composing Drama for Stage and Screen*. Boston, Mass: Allyn and Bacon, 1986.

Lumley, Frederick, *New Trends in 20th Century Drama: A Survey since Ibsen and Shaw*. London: Barrie and Jenkins, 1972.

Lyotard, Jean-Francois. "Answering the Question: What is Postmodernism?" Trans. Regis Durand in *Innovation/Renovation : New Perspectives on the Humanities*, ed. Ihab and Sally Hassan. Madison: University of Wisconsin Press, 1983.

Mbiti, John S. *Concepts of God in Africa*. New York: Praeger, 1970.

Ngugi, Wa Thiong'o *Homecoming: Essays on African and Caribbean Literature, Culture and Politics*. New York: Lawrence Hill, 1972.

Peterson. Londson, ed. *Black Theatre: A 20th Century Collection of the Work of Its Best Playwrights*. New York: Dodd, Mead, 1971.

Reiter, Seymour *World Theater: The Structure and Meaning of Drama*. New York Dek, 1973.

Scheander, Catherine. *They Found a Way: Lorraine Hansberry*. Chicago, 1978.

Schiff, Ellen. *From Stereotype to Metaphor: The Jew in Contemporary Drama*. Albany: State University of New York Press, 1982.

Simons, John. *Uneasy Stages: A Chronicle of the New York Theatre 1963-1973*. New York: Random House, 1975.

Smith, Barbara. *Towards a Black Feminist Criticism*. New York: Out & Out Books, 1977.

Tate, Claudia, ed. *Black Women Writers at Work*. New York: Continuum, 1983.

Volosinov, V.N. (Mikhail Bakhtin). *Marxism and the Philosophy of Language*. New: York Seminar Press, 1973.

Washington. Mary Helen. *Black-Eyed Susans: Classic Stories by and about Black Women*. New York: The Anchor Books, 1975.

Weales, Gerald. *The Jumping Off Place: American Drama in the 1960s*. London: Macmillan, 1969.

Wilkerson, Margaret B., ed. *9 Plays by Black Women*. New York: New American Library, 1986.

Williams, Mance. *Black Theatre in the 1960s and 1970s*. Westport, Conn: Greenwood Press, 1985.

Williams, Raymond. *Drama from lbsen to Brecht*. Second Rev. Ed. London: Chatto and Windus, 1968.

Woolf, Virginia. *A Room of One's Own*. New York: Harcourt, Brace, Jovanowich, 1957.

Periodicals

Anderson, Mary Louise. "Black Matriarchy: Portrayals of Women in Three Plays," *Black American Literature Forum*. Vol. 10, Spring 1976. 93-94.

Bambara, Toni Cade. "For Colored Girls—And White Girls Too," *MS*. 5, September 1976: 38.

Brown-Guillory, Elizabeth. "Contemporary Black Women Playwrights: A View from the Other Half," *Helicon Nine: 'The Journal of Women's Arts and Letters*. Nos. 14 & 15, 1986: 121.

______. "Black Women Playwrights: Exorcising Myths," *Phylon Quarterly*, Vol. XLVIII, No. 3, 1987: 229-38.

Brown, Lloyd, W. "Lorraine Hansberry as Ironist: A Reappraisal of *A Raisin in the Sun*," *Journal of Black Studies*. Vol. 4, March 1974. 34-37.

Bullins, Ed. "Manifesto," *Village Voice*, Nov. 1973: 60.

Carter, Steven. R. "The John Brown Theatre: Lorraine Hansberry's Cultural Views and Dramatic Goals," *Freedomways*, Fourth Quarter, 1979: 186.

Childress, Alice. "The Negro Woman in American Literature. " *Freedomways*, Vol. 6, First Quarter, 1966: 19.

Christian, Barbara. "The Contrary Women of Alice Walker: A Study of *Love and Trouble*," *The Black Scholar*, 12, Mar.-Apr. 1981: 21-30.

Cixous, Helene. "The Laugh of the Medusa," *Signs*, 1976:46.

Farrison, W. Edward. "Lorraine Hansberry's Last Dramas," *College Language Association Journal*, Vol. 16, No. 2, Dec. 1972: 188-97.

Flowers, Sandra Hollins. "Colored Girls: Textbook for the Eighties," *Black American Literature Forum*, Vol. 15, Summer 1981: 52.

Hansberry, Lorraine. *New York Times*, June 25, 1967.

______. "The Negro Writer and His Roots: Toward a New Romanticism," *Black Scholar*, 12.2, 1981: 212.

Iglehart, Hallie. "Unnatural Divorce of Spirituality and Politics," *Quest*, 4, 3, Summer 1978: 20-22.

Issacs, Harold. "Five Writers and Their African Ancestors," *Phylon*, Vol. 21, Fourth Quarter, 1960, 237-84.

Kolodny, Annette. "Critical Response: The Feminist as Literary Critic," *Critical Inquiry*, 2, Summer 1976, 824-25.

Lerner, Max. "The Limbo Plays," *New York Post*, November 2, 1964: 52-56.

Lester, Neal A. "Shange's Men: *For Colored Girls*, Revisited and Movement Beyond," *African-American Review*, Vol. 26, No. 2, 322.

Mapp, Edward. "Black Women in Films," *The Black Scholar*, Vol. 13, Summer 1982: 37.

Miller, E. Ethelhert. "For ZAKI—Who Dances the Bomba," *New Directions*, April 1980: 30.

Milner, Ron. "Black Theatre—Go Home," *Negro Digest*, April 1968, reprinted in Gayle, *Black Aesthetic*. 291.

Molette, Barbara. "Black Women Playwrights: They Speak Who Listens?" *Black World*, Vol. 25, April 1976: 28-34.

Oliver, Edith. "The Theatre/Off-Broadway A Photograph and Where the Missisippi Meets the Amazon," *New Yorker*, 2 Jan 1978: 48.

Powell, J. Bertie. "The Blacks Experience in Margaret Walker's Jubilee and Lorraine Hansberry's *The Drinking Gourd*," *College Language Association Journal*, Vol. XXI, No. 2, Dec. 1977: 304-11.

Ramanan, Mohan. "Who is Afraid of Absurdity?: The Intellectual in Lorraine Hansberry's *The Sign in Sidney Brustein's Window*," *Indian Journal of American Studies: Special Issue on African-American Women Writers*, Vol. 20, No. 1, Winter 1990: 67-73.

Rich, Frank. "Theatre: 'Raisin in the Sun' Anniversary in Chicago," *New York Times*, October 5, 1983: C24.

Richards, David. "Shining 'Raisin in the Sun': At the Eisenhower, a Powerful Production of a Great American Play," *Washington Post*, Nov. 17, 1986, D1, D8.

Richards, Sandra L. "Conflicting Impulses in the Plays of Ntozake Shange," *Black American Literature Forum,* Vol. 17, Summer 1983: 73.

Shange, Ntozake. *Southern Register*, 5, Spring/Summer 1985.

Smith, Barbara. "Towards a Black Feminist Criticism," *Conditions Two*, 1, October 1977: 32.

Smith, Yvonne. "Ntozake Shange: A Colored Girl Considers Success." *Essence*, Feb. 1982: 12+

Staples, Robert. "The Myth of Black Macho: A Response to Angry Black Feminists," *Black Scholar*, Mar.-Apr. 1979, 24-33.

Trescott, Jaqueliine. "Ntozake Shange: Searching for Respect and Identity," *Washington Post,* 29 June 1976: B5.

Weales, Gerald. "Thoughts on *A Raisin in the Sun*," *Commentary*, Vol. XXVII, No. 6, June 1959, 527-30.

Wilkerson, Margaret. "The Sighted Eyes and Feeling Heart of Lorraine Hansberry," *Black American Literature Forum,* Vol. 17, Spring 1983, 11-66.

______. "Lorraine Hansberry: The Complete Feminist," *Freedomways*, Vol. 19, Fourth Quarter, 1979, 188-89.

Index